Ruhlman's

HOW TO
ROAST

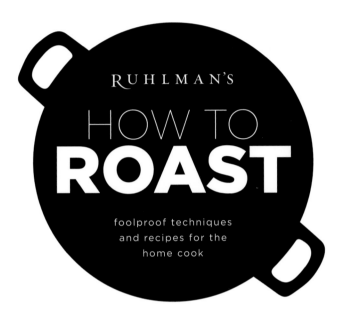

RUHLMAN'S

HOW TO
ROAST

foolproof techniques
and recipes for the
home cook

MICHAEL RUHLMAN

photographs by donna turner ruhlman

LITTLE, BROWN AND COMPANY

NEW YORK BOSTON LONDON

Little, Brown and Company
Hachette Book Group
1290 Avenue of the Americas, New York, NY 10019
littlebrown.com

First Edition: October 2014

Little, Brown and Company is a division of Hachette Book Group, Inc.
The Little, Brown name and logo are trademarks of Hachette Book Group, Inc.

The publisher is not responsible for websites (or their content) that are not owned by the publisher.

ISBN 978-0-316-25410-6
Library of Congress Control Number 2014940623

10 9 8 7 6 5 4 3 2 1

Design: Level, Calistoga, California

SC

Printed in China

For Peter Stevenson

CONTENTS

THE MOST IMPORTANT THING I LEARNED IN COOKING SCHOOL

WHEN I ENTERED THE CULINARY INSTITUTE OF AMERICA as a journalist to write a book about learning to cook professionally, I became one of its best students ever. Not because I was smarter or more talented than anyone else, but because of the unusual nature of my long immersion as a non-student. I was there to find out what the oldest and most prominent cooking school in the country thought one had to know to be a chef, and to convey this through story, which required characters, conflict, dialogue, action.

In order to get this story, I had to take notes all but continuously. If I wasn't chopping or sautéing, I was scribbling in a notebook. I recorded interviews with chefs and transcribed them. Every night I returned home and typed out all my notes, whether they concerned how to make a brown veal stock or the background of the lead characters in my story, which was eventually published as *The Making of a Chef: Mastering Heat at the Culinary Institute of America.* No one took better notes, let alone typed them all out. So not only did I get a good story, but my reporting gave me an in-depth knowledge of the culinary fundamentals, and reinforced both the intellectual and physical skills—the tools—necessary to continue educating myself in the kitchen.

Part of my good fortune was to be placed first thing in a "Skills kitchen" with a young, articulate chef, Michael Pardus. The old way of teaching cooking was this: the apprentice watched the chef and then did as the chef did; if he asked "Why?" the answer was "Because I said so." Here, in the first of all the teaching kitchens at the CIA, we learned why. And we started with the basics—how to hold a knife, how to slice an onion, how to make a stock, and so on. We were always taught the whys of those basics: you grip the blade between the thumb and the first knuckle of your index finger because it gives you maximum control; you first knock out the core when slicing an onion so that all the slices separate; you cook stock not at a simmer but rather at scarcely a bubble, so that fat and other impurities do not emulsify into your stock.

As the seminal chef Auguste Escoffier notes in *Le Guide Culinaire,* referred to at the school as "the bible," nothing of importance can be attempted before you learn the basics. Nothing.

Pardus loved the basics and the whys of cooking. And I loved to spar with him over details, to question his evaluation of my hollandaise sauce or the seasoning of my soup. He liked to be called out and challenged; I believe that's a big part of what made him a great teacher. He thought out loud, and thereby taught us how to *think* as well as how to season our pasta water or clarify a consommé.

In that Skills kitchen, we learned the fundamentals. We followed recipes but only in the service of techniques—and the primacy of technique over recipe was then, and has been to this day, the guiding principle in all that I do in writing about food and in cooking. Chef Pardus often directed us to one recipe or another in the CIA textbook, *The New Professional Chef* (Fifth Edition, a book I still cherish), but it was always in order to illustrate a technique. Therefore, we braised lamb shanks according to the recipe on page 469 (that page in my copy remains dog-eared nearly two decades later), but the point was to learn a technique: *braising*. Braising is used for tough cuts of meat; the meat is first seared to build flavor, add color, and set the protein, and then cooked low and slow in a moist environment so that the collagen, the connective tissue that makes the meat tough, breaks down into gelatin, leaving the meat tender and giving body to the cooking liquid. We learned that these facts applied not only to the lamb shanks on page 469 but also to pork shoulder, osso buco, beef short ribs, or any tough cut of meat.

Likewise, we weren't given a recipe for roasted chicken to prepare for Chef; we were given a chicken so that he could teach us the fundamentals of the technique: *roasting*.

In Skills, after the day's cooking was done and the kitchen clean, Chef Pardus would lecture on the following day's subject, so that we would be intellectually prepared. First step: *think*. What *is* roasting?

Roasting, in the parlance of culinary school, is a dry-heat cooking method. "Dry-heat cooking method" is not just kitchen jargon, but rather a useful distinction. "Dry heat" suggests that, unlike in braising, the ameliorating effect of liquid does not affect the dish. It also means that we're likely using a high temperature, which results in browning. Sautéing is thus considered a "dry heat" cooking method, too; even though you sauté in a fluid (fat), that fluid can reach high temperatures.

"What is the difference between baking and roasting?" Pardus asked our class, all sixteen of us on stools at four stainless-steel tables after a day of cook-

ing. "Today roasting is done in an oven. So is baking. What's the difference?"

This, of course, is an oft-addressed question, and one well suited to the verbal sparring Pardus so enjoyed.

Adam Shepard, who would eventually become a chef and partner in the restaurant Lunetta in Brooklyn, said, "Essentially, they're the same, just different products."

Pardus said, "Nope."

Adam, equally competitive, said, "I thought you were talking about bread and meat."

"We bake bread, but we roast meat, right?" Pardus said to the class. "What do you do to a ham? You *bake* a ham." Pardus concluded: "There is no practical difference. It's a semantic difference."

Adam looked away, Pardus having essentially reiterated what he, Adam, had said in the first place: they're the same, there's no real difference.

Not now, that is. But for most of human history, roasting and baking *were* two distinct techniques. Roasting originally referred only to the cooking of meat over or next to an open fire, usually on some kind of spit. It was considered the only way to cook a joint of meat, as large bone-in cuts were typically referred to.

According to Bee Wilson's excellent *Consider the Fork: A History of How We Cook and Eat,* this exclusive definition of roasting persisted well into the nineteenth century. It wasn't until the Great Exhibition in Great Britain in 1851, writes Wilson, that the notions of roasting and baking were successfully united in a single device, the Improved Leamington Kitchener, which "explicitly offered to combine the twin functions of roasting and baking with a single fire." The availability and prominence of cast iron surely contributed to the Leamington range's adoption, as well as the country's move from wood to coal as the home's main fuel.

Thus it had always been meat that we roasted. Because we didn't (and still don't) turn pieces of fish on a spit before a fire is likely why we have tradition-

ally "baked" fish rather than roasted it. I'm guessing that only recently did we begin to "roast" fish in an oven, when restaurant chefs began calling their fish dishes "roasted." Roasting sounds so much more appealing on a menu.

Indeed, just about every cut of meat, and every vegetable and fruit, sound better roasted than baked. We would never "roast" bread, though, and we don't "roast" a cake. But for just about every other item or preparation that doesn't include eggs or flour, we can use the term "roast." And of all our cooking terms—sautéed, grilled, poached, broiled—I believe "roasted" is the most evocative adjective we can attach to our food, conjuring as it does ideas of deep, rich flavors and delicious browning. We eat in our mind first or, according to the common phrase, "We eat with our eyes first." Seeing a beautiful preparation, such as a perfectly roasted chicken, prepares us to be pleased, as much as what we *call* a dish whets our appetite. We are much more inclined to order the roasted monkfish rather than the baked monkfish, or the roasted chicken rather than the baked chicken, though there is exactly no difference.

So, while there may no longer be a difference in the *act* of baking or roasting, the semantic difference is meaningful and useful.

Here, in this first book in a new series on cooking methods, I will define roasting as a technique that can be applied to meat and fish, to vegetables, and to fruit. Any preparations that rely on eggs or flour (or other cereals and grains) and that are cooked in an oven shall be considered baked. And, as in the CIA's Skills classes, I will offer only a handful of recipes—those that illustrate broader principles that define what is perhaps our most appealing and cherished cooking technique.

RUHLMAN'S
HOW TO
ROAST

THE
BASICS

KNOW YOUR OVEN

When you set your oven to 350°F, do you believe that it is an absolute and uniform measurement of temperature? Or 180°C, for that matter? If you live in Britain, you may turn your oven to gas 4. I have no idea what gas 4 means, but it might be the most honest measurement of the three as it does not refer to a specific temperature but rather denotes a temperature relative to the others on the dial, which is a better description of the relationship between 350°F and 325°F on your oven. Because the truth is, even if you were to cook on the same day that your oven had been professionally calibrated, some spots will be hotter than others. And if you're following a recipe, how do you know that the recipe writer and the recipe tester had properly calibrated their ovens? Maybe *they* were off. Have you ever stopped to consider why we almost always ask for oven temperatures in increments of 25°F? On the Celsius scale, with the infinitely more useful factors of ten, there tends to be slightly more precision, but the same discrepancies apply: we don't know the exact millimeters of mercury a thermometer would read were it positioned in your roasting pan—or even in two different positions in that same pan.

Ah, but you have an oven thermometer? Excellent. How do you know *it* is accurate? (It probably is; I'm just asking.)

Happily we don't need to know the precise, +/– 0.1-degree measurement when we're roasting a leg of lamb or some parsnips. Foods that we roast are generous and easygoing. Temperature and time are more critical for baked goods. Leave a second batch of cookies in for five extra minutes and you've got two different cookies (one may be ruined); do that with a roasted chicken and the difference is not likely to be noticeable. This also reflects the fact that the smaller the food item is, the smaller the window you have in terms of pulling it out of the oven at its moment of perfection.

More important than choosing 350°F/180°C rather than 375°F/190°C is paying attention to the food itself.

What this means cannot be overemphasized. If I am washing salad greens, with my back to the oven, I am still paying attention to that standing rib roast in the oven. If I'm washing greens, it means that dinner is nearly ready and the meat has been roasting for most of my intended cooking time, so if I don't smell deliciousness in the kitchen, my oven is not hot enough. If I smell smoke, I need to pay even more attention and maybe turn around and use my eyes. If my rib roast has been in the oven for only 15 minutes and I hear violent crackling, I'd better check to make sure that the oven is not too hot. I certainly wouldn't pay attention to the recipe in the book I was following because that won't tell me anything about what *my* roast is doing in *my* oven at that moment.

So when you're cooking, you're using all your senses, the most important of which is common sense. And that just means paying attention. If you smell burning and your roast shouldn't be close to done, you need to evaluate. And you should not simply pay attention to today's chicken or pan of root vegetables and then hit the "reset" button in your brain. You should have roasted chicken and root vegetable files in the vault of your cooking experience. What happened last time, and the time before that? What could have been better last time that I can try to achieve this time? This chicken doesn't seem to be nearly as done as the last one, even though they've been in for the same amount of time at the same temperature. Ah, but this is not a two-and-a-half-pound chicken from the farmers' market like last time but rather a four-pounder from the grocery store. This is how, over time, you develop cooking sense. Cooking sense comes from being aware; to be aware we use taste, touch, smell, sound, sight, experience, and common sense over the continuum of our cooking lives. We might never be able to achieve a state of absolute awareness in the kitchen, but if we strive to pay attention, we continually turn up that awareness by degrees each time we apply heat to food.

Now, having addressed your most valuable cooking tool, well protected between your ears, I return to the primary *roasting* tool, the oven. All ovens are different. Get to know your own by paying attention to how it cooks food. Some ovens run hot, some cool. Some ovens are very hot on the bottom and considerably cooler in the upper racks, while others are more uniform. (As a rule, just about all ovens are hotter at the bottom than at the top, even if you are using a convection oven, which blows the air around and generally cooks hotter—but more about that later.)

While working on the *Bouchon Bakery* cookbook by Thomas Keller and company, executive pastry chef Sebastien Rouxel continuously advised us, "Know your oven." This dictum was underscored when he had to duplicate the bakery's recipes in lead recipe writer and tester Susie Heller's kitchen. She and her colleague Amy Vogler also told me many times, "Know your oven."

A great way to evaluate your oven, I learned from Susie, is to buy some Pillsbury biscuits—the kind that come in a tube. Divide the biscuits between two baking sheets and bake them on lower and upper racks exactly according to the package instructions, which have been heavily tested. When they've baked for the allotted time, take them out and you can see where your oven is hottest. There may not be anything you can do to even out the temperature, but knowing where the hot spots are can spare you from burning cookies and remind you of the need to rotate your baking trays.

But, generally speaking, "Know thy oven" means paying attention to how it has behaved in the past, knowing where the hot spots are, understanding how your particular convection fan works, and so on. Implicit in the command is not to be overly dependent on a recipe. Common sense should almost always override a recipe instruction.

HIGH HEAT

High heat—400°F/200°C and above—is the predominant form of heat used for roasting, whether whole roasts or cut-up vegetables. These high temperatures result in browning, creating the rich, complex flavors we associate with roasted foods. Technically called the Maillard reaction, browning happens when amino acids and other molecules and compounds are transformed by heat. Caramelization, the browning of sugar, can also occur at these high temperatures. But, for the most part, Maillard browning accounts for the deep complexity of flavor in roasted meats and vegetables.

Maillard browning, according to food science expert Harold McGee, begins as low as 250°F/120°C, not much hotter than boiling water. So, while we can brown foods in a low oven, it happens most rapidly and the reactions are most dramatic at high temperatures. The evaporation point of water is important in all cooking. Anything cooking in water cannot brown; anything with abundant water in it, such as the skin of a chicken, won't brown until most of that water cooks off. Thus, for very wet items, such as poultry skin and pretty much all vegetables and fruits, we typically roast at high temperatures. The intense heat (radiating from the oven walls and circulating via convection) dehydrates the food quickly so that browning can occur and heat can move through the food to cook it.

MEDIUM HEAT

I'm calling temperatures between 325°F/165°C and 375°F/190°C medium heat. These temperatures are hot enough to bring about both Maillard browning and the caramelization of sugars. However, the heat is not quite as intense as high heat and is best suited for items that are very dense or need to cook for a long time but might burn in high heat before being cooked through, such as larger root vegetables. (Medium heat is what's primarily used for baking.)

LOW HEAT

At the lowest end of the "low heat" spectrum—which I'm defining as 225°F/110°C to 300°F/150°C—little or no browning will occur, so the cooking doesn't generate new or complex flavors and is essentially just dehydrating the item very slowly. Low heat would typically be used to finish a dish, after high-heat roasting had created desirable browning. Browning begins at 250°F/120°C, which is an effective cooking temperature for large roasts and for highly controlled roasting. If you were to cook a large roast at high heat only, it would be overcooked on the outside layer, perfectly cooked midway in, and raw at the center.

CONVECTION COOKING

Look up "convection" in the dictionary and you'll find the con-fusing (unless you're a scientist) information that the word refers to heat transfer within a fluid. All that's really important for cooks to know is that convection means *movement;* in an oven it refers to the movement of hot air over the food. There are convection currents in all ovens, but a true convection oven uses a fan to blow the hot air around inside the oven. Often there's also a heating coil in the back of the oven that directs additional heat at the food. Using the convection function on your oven is like raising the temperature by 25°F/12°C, which means that you'll want to set your convection oven for 25°F/12°C less than what is called for in a recipe written for a standard oven. The moving air has the effect of eliminating hot spots to some extent, and the currents also sweep away the moisture evaporating off the food. Evaporation has a cooling effect, so using convection reduces the impact of that cooling and increases the speed of dehydration and of Maillard browning.

SPECIALTY ROASTING
(Spit, Pan, Smoke, *Pôelé*)

• **SPIT ROASTING** (see page 75) is the original form of roasting. For most of the history of cooking in the west, up until the mid-1800s, roasting big cuts of meat meant turning the meat in front of a blazing fire by hand, until clever contraptions using weights and gears were invented to perform the work. Today we refer to such a setup as a rotisserie. Indeed, the word derives from the Old French *rostisserie,* a shop that sold roasted meats.

Today, when you see meat turning on a spit at a restaurant before a wall of flames, that's true roasting, roasting in the oldest tradition. Donna and I built a large fire pit on our patio and bought a fifty-dollar motorized spit, and I can attest that spit roasting over a fire is indeed an excellent way to cook a large joint of meat.

• **PAN ROASTING** (see pages 59 and 65) refers to a practice that's common in restaurants and should be encouraged at home because it's such an effective cooking method. In pan roasting, meat is seared in a sauté pan on the stovetop and then the pan is slid into a hot oven to finish cooking.

This method is used for thick but tender items, such as a pork tenderloin, that cook more evenly in a hot oven once a tasty sear has been put on the exterior. It also has the advantage of clearing the stovetop and freeing up the cook to work on other parts of the meal.

• **SMOKE ROASTING** As elaborate grills and smokers proliferate, we hear more about smoke roasting (see page 69). While it's somewhat arbitrary—you could also call it smoking or grilling, depending on the equipment you're using—it's a meaningful designation. Smoke roasting is the cooking of meat at roasting temperatures (250°F/120°C or higher) in a smoky environment, whether it's in a covered charcoal grill over indirect heat or in a proper smoker, using wood for smoke and some additional element for heating the chamber. Big cuts of tough pork are especially fine when smoke roasted at lower temperatures, becoming tender in the heat and picking up the flavorful hardwood or fruitwood smoke.

• **POÊLÉING** The final form of roasting is rarely referred to, and few home cooks know what it means unless they are devotees of Julia Child's *Mastering the Art of French Cooking*, which includes several recipes using this technique. It's called *poêlé* (see page 41), pronounced "pwah-LAY," and it's often described as "butter roasting" (Child translated it as "casserole roasting," which makes sense, too, since it's named after a French word for skillet). What defines the technique is that the meat is cooked in an enclosed vessel with vegetables and butter. Because there's no additional liquid and the meat rests on the vegetables, it's considered a roasting technique rather than a braise, which is defined by the presence of plentiful liquid.

Poêléing is most commonly associated with white meats, especially larger cuts that benefit from a long time in the steamy aromatic enclosure. A capon or large chicken is an excellent candidate for this technique, but veal and pork also yield terrific results. Since the meat is basically steamed in an enclosed pot for most of its cooking, it won't brown unless you put some high heat to it. Most recipes call for browning the meat first, though it could also be done afterward, under a broiler, while you make a sauce using the vegetables on which the meat rested.

THE RECIPES

THE ICON:
ROASTED CHICKEN

THERE SHOULD BE LITTLE DOUBT WHAT RECIPE I WOULD choose to launch a book called *How to Roast*. The roasted chicken is an iconic dish, the preparation most often named by chefs as their favorite meal, I'd wager. It's a dish that says home cooking more than any other, a dish that is accessible to all, a dish that is so revered and appreciated it is often reserved for the special Sunday meal, but one that is so easy it can be a regular week-night dinner. It's ultimately nothing more than a heat-and-serve item. Put it in a pan and put it in the oven. Return in an hour, *et voilà!* A perfectly roasted chicken every time.

I made waves in the foodie world a while back, much to my photographer's embarrassment, when I suggested that couples should couple whilst the bird cooks. I had thrown this idea out there rather impetuously, in a blog post (a form of opinion writing that is by nature impetuous), under the headline "America: Too Stupid to Cook." I've long been frustrated by the onslaught of recipes and books promising fast and easy meals, and by the advertisements from companies producing precooked meals packed in plastic, which imply through their focus on fast and easy that cooking real food is slow and difficult. It's no wonder that the processed food purveyors want you to think that cooking is hard and that if you just buy a can of chicken broth or a boxed cake mix your miserable life will suddenly be clover and rainbows.

The Wednesday food sections and the television shows recycle this harmful notion that cooking is hard, bombarding us with "Here's how we're going to help you pull a fast one on the evil drudgery of cooking your own food." The worst part is that they should, and do, know better. So I posted my diatribe under a photo of the classic home-cooked meal, a roasted chicken. We roast a chicken in our house most weeks, and Donna had been moved to photograph one recently when I'd pulled the bird, juices crackling in the cast-iron pan, from the oven, so inviting it was to her, so delicious-looking.

In a bit of a satire, I followed up my diatribe with "The World's Most Difficult Roasted Chicken Recipe." Ostensibly concerned that my too-stupid-to-cook readers were also too unimaginative to figure out what to do with this big free hour they had while the bird was in the oven, I offered suggestions. I also suggested this publicly at an IACP conference—to much tittering, I discovered later when I watched the clip on YouTube. And then an editor at *The New Yorker*, who was compiling a book of essays and recipes from men who cook, asked me to explore this idea, as there was indeed growing evidence of the social benefits of cooking at home. *Slate* picked up the essay and soon the question "Do you want to roast a chicken?" became a secret handshake-cum-pickup-line in certain foodie circles and a way to flirt on Twitter without the non-foodie spouse's catching on. Or so I like to think.

The point, though, was not to encourage roasting a chicken as an excuse for having sex. The point was that cooking is so easy you can have sex in the middle of a recipe. Yes, time has to pass while the food cooks, but you don't have to stare at the oven all the while. Most importantly, I wanted to proclaim that cooking isn't a hobby you do on the side, but rather an act that might be happily integrated into the fabric of your day.

The icon of home cooking is to me a roasted chicken, a dish that is at the same time both a supremely special preparation and a quintessentially humble one. I shake my head when people ask me for my roasted chicken recipe. The "recipe" is so easy I have to struggle for ideas to make it harder. Somehow, "Put well-salted bird into hot oven for 1 hour; let rest 15 minutes" doesn't really satisfy, though it did take on a life of its own when it involved two people.

All of which is to say that the roasted chicken is many things, both actual and symbolic, and also an emblem of the technique, of what roasting is all about—the high, dry heat and the deep, rich flavors and heady aromas that result.

How to Roast a Chicken

There are, of course, many ways to roast a chicken. High heat or low heat, covered or uncovered, on a bed of aromatic vegetables or unadorned. The weirdest roasted chicken technique I read was one by the Michelin-starred British modernist chef Heston Blumenthal, who roasts the bird at 200°F/95°C—that's below boiling! It all depends on what you're after, and me, I'm after a bird with a juicy breast, hot and tender thighs (is there any wonder Eros is never far from a roasted chicken?), succulent wings, and crisp, salty, golden-brown skin. It also fills the home with delicious aromas, which soothes stress and helps us feel relaxed.

1 (4-pound/1.8-kilogram) chicken, trussed

Kosher salt

SERVES 4

- **PREHEAT** the oven to 450°F/230°C (or 425°F/220°C if you have convection); if your oven hasn't been cleaned recently or your kitchen has bad ventilation, use 425°F/220°C.

- **RINSE** the bird under cold water and let the water drain off. **RAIN** salt down onto the bird, covering it completely.

- **PUT** the bird, breast side up, in an ovenproof skillet or other low-sided pan and **ROAST** it for 1 hour.

- **REMOVE** the bird to a cutting board and **LET** it sit there for 15 to 20 minutes, and then **CARVE** and **SERVE**.

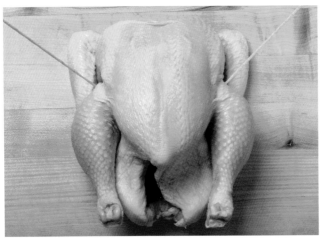

Step 1. Put a 3-foot/1-meter length of butcher's string under the chicken.

Step 2. Cross the string (as if tying a square knot) and pull it taut.

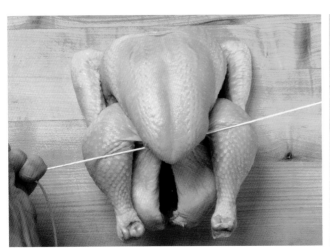

Step 3. This helps ensure a plumped-up breast.

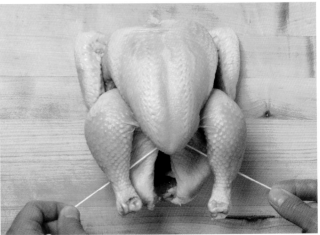

Step 4. Cross the string under the ends of the drumsticks.

Step 5. Loop the string over the drumsticks, then pull tightly so that they overlap.

Step 6. Pull the string around either side of the chicken above the neck.

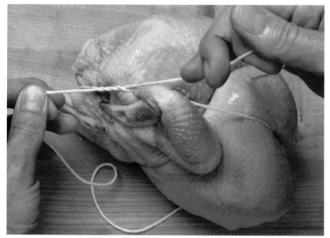

Step 7: Secure the string behind the neck of the bird using a triple loop or slipknot.

Step 8. Cut off excess string (notice the wing tips are folded under the bird).

THE FINER POINTS

WEIGHT

I've learned from experience that a bird of this weight, the weight most commonly available in grocery stores, cooks perfectly in 1 hour. If you're roasting a smaller bird, you can reduce the time to 45 or 50 minutes. If you're not sure whether the bird is done, tilt it so that the juices collecting in its cavity spill out into the pan; if the juices are not pink, remove the bird from the oven; if they're still bloody, check again in 5 minutes. A large bird (one weighing 5 pounds/2.25 kilograms) would be a good candidate for the *poêlé* technique (see page 41).

TRUSSING

A trussed bird (see facing page) looks much lovelier than one untrussed, but the main benefit of trussing a bird is that it cooks more uniformly, preventing the breast from overcooking and drying out. When you truss a bird, you reduce the amount of air circulating in the cavity, which is what overcooks the breast. You can stuff an onion or lemon in the cavity to reduce circulation in lieu of trussing, but these very moist items release a lot of steamy moisture, which may affect the crispiness of the skin. They do have a lovely aromatic effect on the pan juices and fat, though. All of these issues are personal matters for each cook to decide.

SALT

Salting the bird properly is fundamental to its excellence. You want a light but definitive and uniform coating of salt. Some cooks and chefs prefer to salt the bird up to a day ahead and let it sit on a rack in the refrigerator. This dehydrates the skin so that it becomes especially crisp; the salt also begins to penetrate and season the meat. I prefer to salt the bird just before roasting so that it doesn't dissolve and instead gives the skin a coarse texture. Brining the chicken will result in a nicely seasoned bird with a smooth and shiny brown skin—also fine if that's what you prefer. Another recommended flavoring technique is to smear butter and chopped fresh

(continued on page 22)

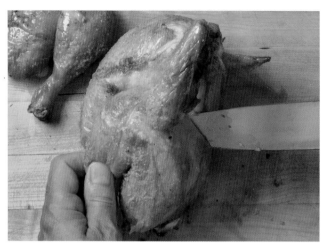

Step 1. Remove the legs by cutting between the leg and the breast.

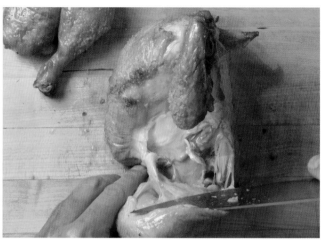

Step 2. Lift the knife blade up and bend the leg back to pop the joint.

Step 3. Separate the wing from the breast.

Step 4. Separate the wing from the wing drumette.

Step 5. To remove the breast, make an incision along the keel bone.

Step 6. Cut through the skin at the tip of the breast.

Step 7. Slice along the rib cage and down over the wishbone, cutting through the joint connecting the wing to the carcass.

The carved bird: two drumsticks, two thighs, two breasts with drumettes attached, two wing flats, and one carcass for stock.

herbs beneath the skin on the breast.

TEMPERATURE

The most critical element of a great roasted chicken is the temperature at which it's roasted. Roasting at high heat ensures crisp skin and perfectly cooked meat—450°F/230°C is optimal. But be warned that animal fat starts smoking at around 350°F/180°C, and at 450°F/230°C not only will the rendered fat be smoking, so too will any previous spills or drips within your oven. So if you're roasting a bird in a studio apartment or haven't cleaned your oven in months, I recommend reducing the heat to 425°F/220°C. This will still result in a satisfactory bird. If you have a vent hood or a well-ventilated kitchen, the smoke inconvenience is worth the payoff of crispy skin, succulent breast, and tender thighs.

If you have the option of using convection, do so. The air currents continuously move the evaporating moisture away from the skin, and this results in better browning and crisping of the skin. Of course the drawback is that the fat in the pan spatters at high heat and the convection currents blow the oil droplets around so that they coat the oven and will smoke quite a bit the next time you roast at high heat if you don't clean your oven in the interim.

BASTING

Sometimes I feel like basting the chicken, if I'm not otherwise occupied. The hot rendered fat facilitates more rendering and an increasingly crisp skin. It's not necessary, but it's fun to do, scooping up the hot fat and watching it sizzle over the skin (the hot fat conducts the oven heat). So, baste once or twice if it pleases you.

RESTING

When the bird has roasted for an hour (give or take 5 minutes either way), the final part of the cooking happens: resting. Its importance cannot be overstated. The bird continues to cook while it rests; neglecting this step can thus mean the difference between a perfectly roasted bird and an unevenly cooked bird.

Remove the bird from the pan (some skin and meat should remain stuck to the pan when you do; this can be peeled away and eaten as a cook's treat while the bird rests, or remain in the pan to flavor a water-and-wine *jus*).

As the bird sits for the next 15 minutes, or up to 25 minutes, the intense heat in the exterior of the chicken will continue to move into the center of the chicken, the temperatures throughout equalizing as the chicken finishes cooking. That's right, the chicken is still cooking as it rests on the cutting board—preferably a cutting board with a moat, as juices will leave the bird during this final stage, and more will run out when the legs are separated from the carcass. If you're making a sauce, add these juices to the pan.

During the resting, complete the remaining dishes of the meal, or make a simple pan sauce. Place the roasting pan with the rendered fat and stuck-on skin over medium-high heat. Sauté a thinly sliced carrot and half a thinly sliced onion until tender. Add 1 cup/240 milliliters dry white wine and reduce it completely; then add 1 cup/240 milliliters water and reduce this by one-third. Strain the sauce through a fine-mesh sieve

or use as is; or, for a richer *jus,* reduce the water completely and repeat as desired until you have a rich, brown, intensely flavorful sauce.

SERVING

To serve, remove the wing flats (another cook's treat, or you can serve them along with the rest of the bird). Remove each leg at the joint connecting it to the carcass, and then separate the drumstick and thigh if you wish. Remove each breast half by slicing down either side of the keel bone, working the knife along the rib cage, and down the wishbone, separating the breast and wing drumette in one piece. Each breast half can then be sliced crosswise, depending on how you want to serve it and how large the breast pieces are.

Spoon the pan sauce over the chicken and serve immediately.

STANDING
RIB
ROAST

BY FAR ONE OF THE MOST SATISFYING AND CELEBRATORY cuts of meat to roast is a rack of beef ribs. It's what our family roasts for Christmas dinner most years, a symbol of abundance and an impressive, delicious centerpiece for a holiday meal. This cut comes from the front rib section of the cow and leads into the strip loin farther down, a leaner but equally delicious roast. The standing rib roast (cut individually for grilling, these become rib-eye steaks) comprises the loin (the main lean muscle), the fat cap (an outer layer of striated meat and fat), intramuscular fat, and rib bones. All of these components come together as a kind of meaty chamber-orchestra suite when properly roasted.

The exterior fat cap will become well done, but it protects the precious inner loin from the dry oven heat, lacing it with such abundant fat that it remains tender and juicy even at high temperatures. The intramuscular fat and ribs, too, help keep everything juicy inside.

The standing rib roast provides an important lesson in roasting: bones temper the harsh, dry heat of the oven. Notice how much rarer the meat is close to the bone than an inch away; the bone tempers the heat, and while the roast rests the hot bone will subtly convey the heat to the meat. Perhaps more importantly, roasted bones are delicious to gnaw on. The late San Francisco chef Judy Rodgers, whom I made no bones about admiring excessively, used to serve roasted duck bones on Halloween at the Zuni Café—a duck skeleton! She would break

When given the choice to roast meat (or fish) with bones or without, always roast on the bone.

down ducks for other cuts but save the bones for pleasure. She'd coat them in oil or fat, add a sprinkling of salt, and roast them at high heat till they looked and smelled too delicious to bear. Yes, you can just roast bones and chew on them, crack them with your teeth if they're small enough, and suck out the marrow. Roasted bones are deeply satisfying, a visceral affirmation of our omnivorous nature.

1 standing rib roast (1 pound/450 grams per person)

Kosher salt

Freshly ground black pepper

- **UNWRAP** the roast, cover it with a light coat of salt, and refrigerate it uncovered for up to 4 days. **REMOVE** it from the refrigerator 6 hours before cooking.

- **PREHEAT** the oven to 450°F/230°C.

- **COVER** the exterior of the roast with pepper. **PLACE** it, rib side down, on a baking sheet lined with parchment paper or in a shallow roasting pan (with or without a rack) and **PUT** it in the oven.

- **REDUCE** the oven temperature to 225°F/110°C and **ROAST** until the internal temperature on an instant-read or cable thermometer reads 120°F/49°C (very rare), 125°F/52°C (rare), or 130°F/54°C (medium-rare), depending on how you like it. This should take about 25 minutes per pound/50 minutes per kilo, give or take. (Convection will speed up the cooking by about 10 minutes per pound/20 minutes per kilo; however, when roasting at low temperatures, I believe that slower is better.)

- **REMOVE** from the oven to a cutting board (preferably one with a moat, to catch the delicious juices) and **LET** it rest for 30 minutes.

- **CARVE** between each rib and **SERVE**.

THE FINER POINTS

SALT

Salt discourages spoilage bacteria and penetrates the muscle. I typically buy the roast 3 to 4 days before I cook it. I salt it the day I buy it and refrigerate it, uncovered, on a baking sheet. (If space is an issue, don't worry; buying it several days ahead is optimal but not required.) I don't cover it because I want the exterior to dry out as much as possible to better facilitate browning.

TEMPERING

Never put a roast straight from the refrigerator into the oven because the outside will become hot long before the chilled center even reaches rare. The roast needs to sit out at room temperature for several hours. If you have a very large roast, it will take several more hours to cook. So plan ahead, working your way backward from the time you intend to serve it: 30 minutes of resting, several hours of roasting, and several hours of sitting at room temperature.

You can use a roasting pan and rack if you wish (it does look pret-tier), but a roast rests on the edges of the ribs and so has air circulating around it regardless of what you cook it in or on. The key is the air circulation, so don't try to roast in a deep pot. I salt, refrigerate, temper, and roast all on the same baking sheet.

TEMPERATURE

There is no single "right" approach to cooking a standing rib roast, though all methods follow a similar rationale. The heat needs to be high enough to let the roast achieve a nicely browned surface, yet low enough—and for long enough—to allow the interior to heat to rare or medium-rare without overcooking the portions of the meat closer to the exterior. Marlene, my colleague and chief recipe tester, cooks a rib roast several times a year. She sometimes uses a high-heat method, which works well but leaves a mess and makes the oven smoke like the devil. The appeal of this method is that it's a faster cook time, so use it if you have time constraints. Pre-

Step 1. Season a standing rib roast with pepper and plenty of salt.

Step 2. A perfectly seasoned rib roast.

Step 3. Having been seasoned several days in advance, the rib roast, on a sheet tray lined with parchment paper, is ready for the oven.

Step 4. To carve the roast, remove the loin from the ribs (reserve the ribs for those who deserve them).

Step 5. Removed from the ribs, the roast can be sliced to whatever thickness you wish.

heat the oven to 500°F/260°C (or 475°F/245°C if you have convection). Put the room-temperature roast in the oven and roast for 5 minutes per pound/10 minutes per kilo, and then turn off the oven. Let the roast finish cooking in the turned-off oven for 90 minutes or, if you're using a cable thermometer, till it reaches the desired temperature. Remove the roast from the oven and let it rest for 15 to 30 minutes. You will be left with an excellent roasted exterior, a beautiful medium-rare interior, and a difficult-to-clean roasting pan and fat-spattered oven. When not pressed for time, Marlene prefers to roast this cut at 225°F/110°C for 25 minutes per pound/50 minutes per kilo.

I don't know who originated the blowtorch method, but I wrote about it with Thomas Keller and Dave Cruz in the cookbook *Ad Hoc at Home*. If you give the exterior a quick blast with a blowtorch before putting it in the oven, it jumpstarts the Maillard reaction (Chef Cruz's method calls for roasting at 275°F/135°C to an internal temperature of 128°F/53°C, about 2 hours per pound/4 hours per kilo). The blowtorch method works for all cuts of meat.

Regardless of what method you use, I strongly urge you to use a digital thermometer to determine doneness. I prefer a cable thermometer that allows me to watch the internal temperature while it cooks.

SERVING

I like to serve a rich roasted beef stock with a standing rib roast, both to keep the meat warm and moist and to flavor other items on the plate (mashed potatoes and/or Yorkshire pudding, for example). To make a rich beef stock, follow the instructions for Brown Veal Stock (page 111), replacing the veal bones with meaty beef bones.

I also prepare a horseradish sauce by folding prepared horseradish into whipped cream and adding some salt and lots of black pepper.

THE
THANKSGIVING
TURKEY

THIS MAY BE THE ONE DISH THAT MORE AMERICANS UNITE IN cooking than any other, and every November seems to arrive with a collective panic about roasting the turkey successfully. The newspaper food sections and cooking blogs bombard us with different takes on cooking the turkey—roasting, deep-frying, grilling, steaming—and the battle over whether to stuff the turkey is waged yet again.

Here I am going to stick with the traditional roasting method—the cavity filled with aromatic herbs, vegetables, and lemon; the bird trussed and salted—and we'll follow the same basic rules for the roasted chicken.

The size of the bird is important. The larger it is, the harder it is to cook properly. That's what makes the turkey challenging, the fear that the breast will dry out before the legs are cooked through and tender. A 20-pound/ 9-kilogram bird is really too big to get just right, so if you must cook a bird this big it's best to use a combination method of roasting and braising. Here I'm restricting the size to 10 to 12 pounds/4.5 to 5.5 kilograms, enough to feed 8 to 10 people.

I grew up in the stuffed-bird tradition and subsequently ate overcooked breast moistened by Grandma Spamer's gravy. (Her stuffing was worth any number of slices of dry breast.) I prefer not to stuff the bird when I prepare it myself; a stuffed bird takes considerably longer to roast, as there's no hot air cooking the bird from within but rather a solid mass of starch. Furthermore, that stuffing will end up having spent much time at warm, bacteria-loving temperatures with egg and poultry juices in it and so needs to be made hot before serving. If you intend to stuff your bird, see "The Finer Points" below the recipe for my recommendations.

The same rules apply to a big turkey as to a smaller chicken: You want to prevent too much air from circulating inside the bird. Stuffing it with celery, onion, lemon, and herbs not only accomplishes this, but these ingredients also help perfume the roasted bird and fill the kitchen with delicious aromas.

I truss the bird for appearance and to further protect the interior.

The most important step in the roasting method I recommend is removing the legs and returning them to the hot oven while the big, fat breast rests. The legs really do benefit from extended cooking, and they're difficult to overcook. Removing the legs and cooking them separately will, of course, ruin your opportunity for a carving-the-bird-at-the-table presentation à la Norman Rockwell. I don't like that method of serving anyhow, because the meat gets cold before half the table is served. But presentation is important, so I recommend roasting the whole bird until the breast is done, presenting it to your guests for their appreciation, and then returning to the kitchen, removing the legs, and putting them back in the oven to finish.

In terms of serving the turkey, you want to make sure it's hot. Hot is key. Moist is also key. Therefore, I serve it in hot moisture. Indeed, I slightly undercook the breast so that it finishes cooking in hot stock. It's a foolproof way to ensure that you are relaxed and composed, and your family and friends can all dig in to hot, juicy turkey. This preparation can even be done up to 4 hours before you want to serve it (keep the legs and thighs in the oven at 200°F/95°C), as everything can be reheated in the hot stock at the end.

1 (10- to 12-pound/4.5- to 5.5-kilogram) turkey

Kosher salt

2 celery ribs, cut into large chunks

½ Spanish onion, quartered

½ lemon, halved again

1 bunch thyme (optional)

1 bunch sage (optional)

½ cup/110 grams butter, melted

1 cup/240 milliliters dry white wine

2 cups/480 milliliters turkey or chicken stock,

preferably homemade

SERVES 10

- About 4 hours before you plan to start roasting, **REMOVE** the turkey from the refrigerator, **RINSE** it, **PAT** it dry, and **LET** it sit at room temperature.

- **PREHEAT** the oven to 425°F/220°C (or 400°F/200°C if you have convection).

- Liberally **SALT** the interior and **JAM** the celery, onion, lemon, and herbs (if using) into the cavity of the bird. **TRUSS** the bird as you would a chicken (see page 16). **RAIN** salt evenly all over the bird. **PUT** the bird in a low-sided pan (or elevated on a rack in a roasting pan; you want plenty of circulation around the bird) and **PUT** it in the oven.

- **ROAST** at that high temperature for 20 minutes. **POUR** the melted butter evenly over the bird and **LOWER** the oven temperature to 375°F/190°C (350°F/180°C convection). Continue to **ROAST** until the breast reaches 155°F/ 68°C, 60 to 90 minutes, depending on your oven and the size of the bird, basting as you wish.

- **REMOVE** the pan from the oven. **SHOW** off the bird to your guests. **BRING** it back to the kitchen. **SLICE** through the skin between the legs and breast. The breast should still be pink, but if it looks cold and raw you can return the entire bird to the oven for 10 more minutes. **PUT** the bird on a large cutting board (preferably with a channel or a depression to hold the bird). **REMOVE** each leg at the joint connecting it to the carcass. I reserve the wings for stock the following day rather than serving them, as they're tough and not terribly meaty.

- **POUR** off the fat and juices from the roasting pan (I reserve the fat to make a roux to thicken stock for gravy, and I add the juice to gravy or stock). **RETURN** the legs to the pan and **RETURN** them to the oven. **ROAST** the legs for at least an additional 45 to 60 minutes; if you intend to leave the legs for longer than an hour, **TURN** the oven down to 200°F/95°C (without convection). The legs will only get better with time and can be left in the oven for up to 4 additional hours; don't worry about the breast, as it will reheat in the stock at the end.

- **REMOVE** the legs from the roasting pan. **PUT** the pan over high heat on the stovetop. **ADD** the wine and **BRING** it to a simmer, scraping up the stuck-on skin and browned juices. **ADD** the broth and **BRING** to a simmer, then **TURN** the heat to low.

- **CARVE** the dark meat from the drumsticks and thighs and **PUT** it in the hot stock in the roasting pan. **REMOVE** each breast half from the turkey (be careful not to tear the skin). Don't worry if the breast is a little pink; this means it will be juicy as it finishes cooking in the hot stock. **CUT** the breast crosswise into ¼- to ½-inch/6- to 12-millimeter slices. **TRANSFER** the pieces to the roasting pan with the stock. **TURN** the burner to high and **BRING** the stock to a simmer. **SIMMER** for a minute or two to ensure that everything is hot, and then **SERVE**.

Step 1. Stuff the turkey's cavity with aromatic vegetables, lemon, and herbs. They will perfume the bird and its juices and prevent the breast from overcooking.

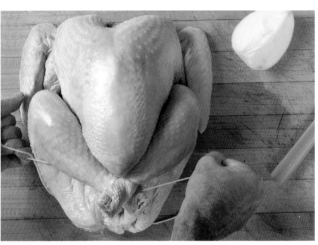

Step 2. Truss the turkey just as you would a chicken (see page 16).

Step 3. Cinch the string tight using the three-times-around method shown for chicken (page 16) or a basic slipknot (see page 45).

Step 4. The trussed turkey, ready to roast in a shallow pan.

THE FINER POINTS

GRAVY

Gravy, a critical part of the Thanksgiving meal, is nothing more than rich turkey stock thickened with flour. To make turkey stock, follow the instructions for Brown Veal Stock (page 111), using turkey wings and necks instead of veal bones. Make the stock ahead of time—several days or even a month in advance—and store it in the freezer. To make gravy, simply sauté a diced onion in butter, add flour (1½ tablespoons per cup/240 milliliters stock), and cook the flour till it smells like piecrust. Whisk in the cold stock until it has thickened and begins to simmer. (For more detailed instructions and photographs, go to Ruhlman.com and search "Thanksgiving gravy.")

STUFFING

I make a turkey *dressing,* in effect a savory bread pudding, using plenty of turkey stock for flavor. I call it a dressing rather than a stuffing because I cook it separately from the turkey. But if you want to go classical, by all means do so. My recommendation is to roast the stuffed turkey as described above (it will take an additional 30 to 60 minutes), remove the stuffing to the roasting pan with the legs, and finish cooking it along with the dark meat until it's piping hot in the center. (For more detailed instructions and photographs, go to Ruhlman.com and search "Thanksgiving dressing.")

WHEN ALL HAVE BEEN SERVED

Relax and enjoy this most special of American holidays.

And be sure to save the carcass for making more stock the next day! Just follow the steps for Brown Veal Stock (page 111), only there's no need to roast the bones, as you've already done it. Simply break up the carcass, cover with water, heat gently for many hours (adding the vegetables and aromatics at the very end), and then strain.

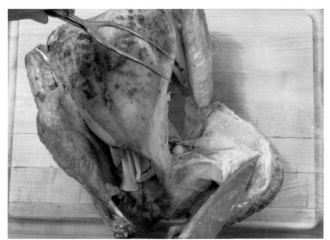

Step 1. When the breast is nearly done, remove the legs as you would from a chicken (page 20).

Step 2. Separate the thigh and drumstick.

Step 3. The roasted turkey, three-quarters cooked.

Step 4. The legs have gotten a longer roast than the breast.

Step 5. When the legs have cooked, remove the breast as you would from a chicken (page 20).

Step 6. Slice along the keel bone, then down over the rib cage and wishbone.

Step 7. Remove both breast halves, reserving the carcass and wings for stock.

Step 8. Slice across the grain so that each piece has some skin.

Step 9. Serve the turkey in the roasting pan in simmering hot stock.

PORC
À LA POÊLE

BUTTER-ROASTED—WHAT A HAPPY TERM! The name of this dish comes from the French verb *poêler,* which means to fry, and anything cooked *à la poêle* is cooked in a frying pan; how it came to denote butter roasting is obscure and may date to Auguste Escoffier, who describes the method in his *Guide Culinaire* of 1903. And while it's rarely used today outside of cooking schools, it's a technique worth noting. The basics are these: a big cut of meat is cooked in a covered pot in a medium oven with lots of aromatic vegetables and plenty of butter.

When I was a boy and pork was still marbled and therefore more flavorful, "pork roast" was a regularly featured meal throughout fall and winter. We "roasted" pork (and chickens) in a covered white-speckled black roasting pan because we didn't know any better. But, lucky for us, pork shoulder is a tough, well-marbled cut that benefited from the hot steamy enclosure, especially when we put a packet of Lipton's onion soup mix on top. Chickens, as noted earlier, are best roasted in high, dry heat. But they, along with larger birds, such as a big capon, are excellent butter-roasted as well, especially when served with the bed of vegetables they cooked on—the leg and thigh are tenderized by the moist heat and the breast doesn't dry out.

Poêléing, or butter roasting, generates its own sauce during the roasting.

The method is midway between roasting and braising. As with braising, there is no browning in the covered pot, with all that cooling moisture inside. Thus we need to start by searing the meat. We then cook the aromatics to whatever degree we wish (just sweated or, for more complexity, browned), return the meat to the pot, cover it, and pop it in the oven. The browning of the aromatics can be done up to 3 days before roasting.

Traditionally, the aromatic vegetables were referred to as *matignon,* which indicated that they were to be eaten along with the meat. And they can be served with the roast if they are not cooked too long (as with a chicken), or you can add wine and water to the pot after cooking the roast and make a pan sauce, straining out and discarding the vegetables. Or, as here, with the roast cooking for a good 90 minutes and releasing a lot of liquid, simply strain out the vegetables, remove the fat that rises, and thicken this perfect sauce with a slurry or *beurre manié.* Because you're straining out the vegetables, it's appropriate to prepare and serve the same type of vegetables afresh, glazed or roasted as you wish.

For this recipe you can use any size roast you wish. I plan on 6 to 8 ounces/ 170 to 225 grams per person when I'm buying the roast, and I figure it will take about an hour to an hour and a half to cook. Unlike pork chops, which I like to serve just over medium-rare, while the meat is still pink and juicy, I think a pork roast should be cooked medium to medium-well. At about 140°F/60°C, it will still be a little tough, so you'll want to slice it thinly. Or take it to 160°F/70°C, which allows the tough muscle time to become tender; because of the marbling in the shoulder, it will still be juicy, like the pork roasts of my youth. I also tie the roast, because it looks better and cooks more evenly. Because of the long cooking time, it's important to choose a well-marbled cut of pork, which is rare in today's supermarket. Try to find a farmer near you who raises pigs; that's all but guaranteed to be better tasting—better on all counts, in fact—and worth the extra cost and effort.

1 (3- to 5-pound/1.35- to 2.25-kilogram) boneless

pork shoulder roast

Kosher salt

1 teaspoon black peppercorns, lightly crushed

in a mortar or beneath a sauté pan

1 teaspoon coriander seeds, lightly crushed

in a mortar or beneath a sauté pan

Vegetable oil

½ cup/110 grams butter

1 Spanish onion, thinly sliced

2 carrots, cut into large dice

5 garlic cloves, gently smashed

1 tablespoon tomato paste

1 bunch thyme, bound with butcher's string

2 tablespoons flour kneaded into 2 tablespoons/30 grams

room-temperature butter *(beurre manié)*

SERVES 6 TO 10

- **PREHEAT** the oven to 350°F/180°C.

- **TIE** the pork roast if you wish. **GIVE** it a uniform coating of salt and then **DUST** the whole thing with the pepper and coriander.

- **COAT** the bottom of a Dutch oven or other covered roasting pan with oil and **PLACE** it over high heat. When the oil is ripplingly hot, **SEAR** all sides of the pork so you have a nice golden brown surface. Take your time.

- **REMOVE** the pork and wipe out the interior of the roasting vessel. **MELT** half of the butter over medium-high heat in the roasting vessel. As it begins to melt, **ADD** the onion, carrots, and garlic. **GIVE** them 2 four-finger pinches of salt and **COOK**, stirring, until the onions are soft and translucent,

10 to 15 minutes. **ADD** the tomato paste and continue to **COOK** and stir until the tomato paste is hot and coats the vegetables. **ADD** the remaining butter and the thyme and **STIR. PUT** the roast on top of the vegetables, **COVER** the vessel, and **PUT** it in the oven until the pork reaches an internal temperature of 140°F/60°C to 160°F/70°C.

- **REMOVE** the pork to a cutting board. If you wish to brown the top of the roast further, **TURN** on the broiler.

- **SET** a strainer over a large measuring cup or medium bowl and **DUMP** the contents of the pot into it. **RETURN** the roast to the pot and **BROIL** it till nicely browned, if you wish, and then **RETURN** the roast to the cutting board.

- When the fat has risen to the top of the juices, **SPOON** it off (use a fat separator if you have one, as there will be lots of fat).

- **POUR** the defatted juices back into the pot and **BRING** to a simmer over medium heat. **WHISK** in the *beurre manié,* a tablespoon at a time, till the sauce is thickened to your liking.

- **SLICE** the pork ¼ to ½ inch/6 to 12 millimeters thick and **SERVE**, spooning the sauce over the top.

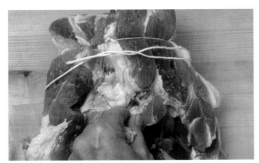

Step 1. A slipknot you can cinch tight is like a backwards square knot.

Step 2. Begin as if you're tying your shoe.

Step 3. Pull the string tight.

Step 4. Wrap the string in your left hand *over* the string in your right.

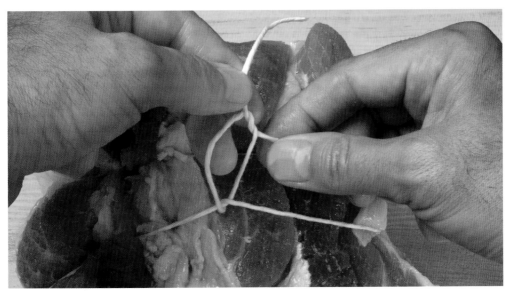

Step 5. Then carry it all the way through the loop.

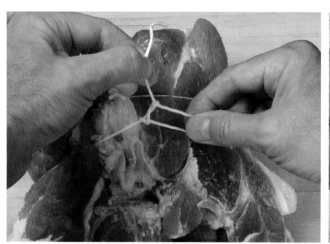

Step 6. Hold the string now in your left hand steady and pull on the string in your right.

Step 7. Pull the knot taut, then release the string in your right hand.

Step 8. Pulling on the string in your left hand, press the knot down with your right to tighten it, then tie it off again to secure it.

Step 9. A boned pork shoulder tied for roasting.

Step 10. The shoulder, seared and ready to braise with herbs and aromatic vegetables.

HALIBUT
WITH BROWNED BUTTER AND LEMON

MEATY HALIBUT CAN BE COOKED USING VIRTUALLY ANY method—grilled, sautéed, poached, or even made into ceviche—but the surest way to cook a thick fish perfectly is to roast it. When some friends sent us a beautiful side of Alaskan halibut, I cut it into 2-inch-thick steaks. I put the steaks, skin side down, in a pan that had preheated inside the hot oven and roasted them for 10 minutes. The fish emerged with a delicate, almost creamy texture, thanks to the even, ambient heat.

Because the fish was so fresh and pristine, I wanted to keep it simple, so I just spooned browned butter over it and finished it with a little squeeze of lemon. Roasted halibut goes beautifully with any number of side dishes but is pictured here with a refreshing black bean salad with summer vegetables and a citrus vinaigrette.

4 (2-inch-/5-centimeter-thick) halibut fillets,

preferably with skin on (about 1½ pounds/680 grams)

Fine sea salt

Vegetable oil

½ cup/110 grams butter

4 lemon wedges

SERVES 4

- **PUT** an ovenproof sauté pan or skillet (cast iron works well) in the oven and **PREHEAT** the oven to 400°F/200°C. (Because fish musculature is so quick to dry out, I don't use convection for any roasted fish.) At the same time, **REMOVE** the fish from the refrigerator and **SET** it, skin side down, on a paper towel–lined plate. **SEASON** the fillets with salt.

- When the oven and pan are hot, **REMOVE** the pan from the oven and **ADD** just enough vegetable oil to coat the bottom; **RETURN** the pan to the oven for a minute or two to heat the oil.

- **REMOVE** the pan and **LAY** the halibut, skin side down, in it. **RETURN** the pan to the oven and **ROAST** until a cake tester, paring knife, or skewer inserted into the center of the fillet feels warm—not cold or hot—against the skin below your lip or on your inner wrist, about 10 minutes.

- While the halibut is cooking, **MELT** the butter in a small sauté pan over medium-high heat. It will sizzle until all of the water has cooked off; once it quiets and turns to foam, **REMOVE** the pan from the heat. It should be nicely browned (**COOK** it a little longer if it's not, but be careful not to burn it).

- **REMOVE** each fillet to a plate (you can serve the fish with the skin or you can slide your spatula between the skin and meat and serve only the meat). **SPOON** the browned butter over each fillet and **SERVE** with a lemon wedge.

Black Bean Salad

This is one of my go-to warm-weather salads for big gatherings and potluck events. Its great versatility, visual appeal, and dynamic vinaigrette make it a real crowd pleaser.

3 ears corn, husked

1 pound/450 grams dried black beans,
soaked and cooked as you wish

1 red bell pepper, seeded and cut into small dice

½ red onion, cut into small dice and rinsed
under hot water for 30 seconds

3 scallions, thinly sliced on the bias

¼ cup/60 milliliters olive oil

3 garlic cloves, minced

1 (1-inch/2.5-centimeter) piece ginger, grated

1 tablespoon ground coriander

2 teaspoons ground cumin

1 teaspoon cayenne pepper, or more to taste

1 teaspoon kosher salt, or more to taste

Juice of 1 lime, or more to taste

Chopped fresh cilantro (optional)

SERVES 12 to 15

- **BRING** a large pot of water to a boil over high heat and **PREPARE** an ice bath. **BLANCH** the corn for 2 minutes and **REMOVE** to the ice bath to chill thoroughly.

- In a large bowl, **COMBINE** the beans, bell pepper, onion, and half of the scallions. **STAND** each ear of corn, narrow end down, in the center of the bowl and **SLICE** off the kernels with a sharp knife, keeping the planks of corn intact as they come off the cob if possible.

- To make the vinaigrette, **COMBINE** the olive oil, garlic, ginger, coriander, cumin, and cayenne in a sauté pan over medium-high heat and **COOK**, stirring, until the garlic and ginger are lightly fried (about 30 seconds after the water in the butter begins vaporizing).

- **POUR** the spiced oil over the beans and vegetables and **TOSS** to coat. **ADD** the salt and stir in the lime juice. **TASTE** and **EVALUATE** for acidity, seasoning, and flavor. **ADD** more lime juice, salt, and/or cayenne till it pleases you.

- **GARNISH** with the remaining scallions and the cilantro (if using) and **SERVE** immediately, or **CHILL** and **SERVE** later.

ROASTED **SHELLFISH** WITH TARRAGON AND THYME BROTH

NOT ONLY IS ROASTING A FABULOUS METHOD FOR PREPARING a variety of mollusks and crustaceans, it also encourages the use of a communal platter, one of my favorite ways to share a meal. It's a festive sight, and it encourages festivity in the way you eat it. It's also very easy.

You can use any shellfish that happens to look good. For this dish I found very good shellfish at my nearby Whole Foods Market. Be aware, though, that very large clams or quahogs will take a few minutes longer than the other items, so you may want to throw them into the roasting pan a couple of minutes before the rest. I like to cook the shrimp in the shells because they come out tenderer; I also like having to peel them to eat them (but if you are finicky about eating with your hands, you can add peeled shrimp at the very end, so that they cook as you finish the sauce).

The following recipe serves two, but it's easy to scale it up. For each person, plan on about 5 mussels, 5 littleneck clams, 3 larger clams, half a small lobster tail, and 3 shrimp. Use one skillet or two as needed, allowing the shellfish to be fairly close together but not stacked high on top of each other. And remember that you'll be serving this at the table, so choose pans that will look good there and be easy to serve from (low-sided round skillets rather than a high-sided rectangular roasting pan, though the latter would be fine for a large group).

10 mussels

10 littleneck or cherrystone clams

6 top neck clams or quahogs

1 (4-ounce/115-gram) lobster tail, halved lengthwise

6 medium shrimp

Olive oil

2 garlic cloves, minced

1 shallot, minced

¼ cup/60 milliliters dry white wine

1 small bunch thyme

5 leafy tarragon sprigs

¼ cup/60 grams butter, cut into 4 pieces

Freshly ground black pepper

SERVES 2

- **PUT** your roasting pan or pans in the oven and **PREHEAT** the oven to 450°F/230°C—you can go as high as 500°F/260°C if your oven is clean (otherwise you'll have lots of smoke!).

- **SOAK** the mollusks in cold water and **BRUSH** their shells thoroughly under cold running water to wash off as much sand and grit as possible.

- **COMBINE** all of the shellfish in a large bowl and **TOSS** with enough olive oil to lightly coat them all. **DUMP** them into the hot pan or pans and **ROAST** for a few minutes (if using very large clams, **ADD** these first and **ROAST** them for 2 minutes before adding the remaining items). **STIR** or **TOSS** the shellfish to redistribute them. Just before the lobster and shrimp are cooked through—8 to 10 minutes total cooking time; the lobster should be firm but not rubbery—**REMOVE** the pan from the oven and **SET** it over a hot burner. The mollusks will have released liquid upon opening. **BRING** this liquid to a simmer over medium-high heat. **PUSH** the shellfish to the side and **ADD** the garlic and shallot. **COOK** for 20 to 30 seconds, and then **ADD** the wine and the herbs. **BRING** the liquid back to a simmer and **WHISK** in the butter, tablespoon by tablespoon, until it's melted. **GRIND** some pepper into the broth. **TOSS** the shellfish so that everything is nicely cooked and coated with the broth. **DISCARD** any mollusks that haven't opened.

- I like to pour the shellfish broth into large bowls and then let everyone serve themselves. **SET** out additional bowls as needed for shells. Corn on the cob is delicious when steamed or boiled and then rolled in the salty shellfish broth. **SERVE** some crusty bread to soak up the broth.

The mollusks release plentiful liquid in the high heat as they roast. Mounting butter into the liquid with herbs creates a fabulous sauce.

PAN-ROASTED
RACK OF LAMB

MANY HIGH-HEAT TECHNIQUES THAT ARE UBIQUITOUS IN restaurant kitchens ought to be more universally embraced at home, foremost among them pan roasting. It's a simple, effective method in which you start a piece of meat or fish in a skillet on the stovetop and finish it in the oven. In restaurants, it's a matter of efficiency: Putting the pan in the oven frees up valuable burner space. The same holds true at home, but I've found that even when I don't have six pans vying for the stovetop, just getting the main item out of the way makes finishing the rest of the dinner easier.

I like to baste the meat as it roasts with a flavorful fat—here, it's butter and rendered lamb fat flavored with garlic and thyme.

Basting not only flavors the meat, but it also helps it to cook uniformly. My go-to baste for red meat is simply butter with a bunch of thyme and a few smashed garlic cloves; the butter takes on the flavor of the thyme and garlic and herb as it browns.

Step 1. The pan-roasted rack of lamb is finished with butter.

Step 2. Basting the lamb helps to flavor it and cook it evenly.

Step 3. Let the lamb rest out of the pan for 15 to 20 minutes.

Step 4. Slice the rack into two-rib cuts to serve.

1 (8-rib) rack of lamb, frenched

Vegetable oil

Kosher salt

1 teaspoon black peppercorns,

lightly crushed in a mortar or beneath a sauté pan

1 teaspoon coriander seeds,

lightly crushed in a mortar or beneath a sauté pan (optional)

5 garlic cloves, gently smashed

¼ cup/60 grams butter

1 bunch thyme

SERVES 4

- **REMOVE** the lamb from the refrigerator about 4 hours before you intend to cook it.

- **PREHEAT** the oven to 425°F/220°C.

- **RUB** the lamb all over with 1 tablespoon oil. **COAT** the lamb with salt. **SPRINKLE** it evenly with the pepper and, if using, the coriander.

- **POUR** enough oil into an ovenproof skillet, appropriate to the size of your lamb rack, so that it coats the bottom. **HEAT** the oil over high heat until shimmering. **PUT** the lamb, fat side down, in the pan and **SEAR** till the surface is nicely browned, a few minutes. **TURN** the lamb so the fat side is up and the bone side is down and **PUT** the skillet in the oven.

- After 5 minutes, **REMOVE** the pan from the oven and **POUR** off the oil. **ADD** the garlic and butter. **MELT** the butter by either putting the pan over high heat on the stovetop or returning it to the oven for a couple of minutes. When the butter is melted, **ADD** the thyme and **BASTE** the lamb with the butter.

- **PUT** the lamb back in the oven and **ROAST** until a thermometer inserted in the center of the loin reads 128°F/53°C, basting two or three more times along the way (this will give you medium-rare lamb; 130°F/54°C will give you medium). The lamb should take 15 to 20 minutes to cook in the oven. **LET** it rest for 15 to 20 minutes before cutting.

- **SERVE** on top of or with Roasted Root Vegetables (page 103) or, in spring, a sauté of asparagus, corn, and onion.

Sautéed Asparagus with Corn and Onion

- **BLANCH** and **SHOCK** a bunch of asparagus. **SLICE** off the tips, and then **CUT** the asparagus into coins the size of corn kernels. **BLANCH** and **SHOCK** 2 ears of corn and then **REMOVE** the corn from the cob, leaving as many planks of corn intact as possible.

- In a medium sauté pan, **MELT** 1 tablespoon butter over medium-high heat. **ADD** ½ Spanish onion, diced, and **GIVE** it a four-finger pinch of kosher salt. When the onion is tender, 3 or 4 minutes, **ADD** the asparagus and corn to heat through. **ADD** ½ cup/120 milliliters Brown Veal Stock (page 111) if you have it on hand.

PAN-ROASTED **MONKFISH** ON A BED OF GARLICKY TOMATOES AND BASIL

BECAUSE IT'S A FAT, MEATY FISH, MONKFISH IS AN EXCELLENT candidate for roasting. The ambient heat of the oven ensures uniform cooking of the fish. Monkfish is also very forgiving; it stays juicy even if you overcook it (but don't, if you can help it). And, unlike thinner fish, monkfish can rest and finish cooking, while you make the sauce, without becoming cold or dry. It sometimes comes with a tough outer membrane or silver skin, which you should remove if your fishmonger hasn't already done so. It also has a single spine that runs down half the tail. I prefer to cook it with the bone removed for easier slicing; if you like, it can be roasted with the bone in.

The sauce, made from fresh tomatoes and basil, is one of my favorite all-purpose sauces for use on mild fish and white meat, and especially on pasta. It takes advantage of salt's capacity to extract copious water out of the tomatoes. This flavorful tomato water is strained into the same pan the fish roasted in and then mounted with butter to create an excellent sauce base. The fish can be returned to the pan when the sauce is hot to keep it warm if you wish.

A cake tester is an excellent tool to determine if the fish is done; it should feel warm, not cold or hot, after being inserted into the thickest part of the fish.

2 large beefsteak tomatoes (or similarly large, juicy tomatoes), diced

1 teaspoon kosher salt

1 whole monkfish tail, bone and tough silver skin removed

Olive oil

Fine sea salt

4 garlic cloves, minced

¼ cup/60 grams cold butter, cut into 4 pieces

10 to 12 fresh basil leaves, cut into a chiffonade

SERVES 4

- **PREHEAT** the oven to 425°F/220°C.

- **PUT** the diced tomatoes in a bowl and **SPRINKLE** half of the kosher salt over them. **TOSS** and then **SPRINKLE** the remaining kosher salt over them. The water extraction will take at least 10 minutes and can be done up to an hour before you begin to cook.

- **TIE** the monkfish tail with butcher's string to secure the fatter end, where the bone has been removed, and to make the fish more compact for even cooking. **RUB** it with olive oil and **DUST** it evenly with fine sea salt. **PLACE** it in a large skillet and **PUT** it in the oven until it reaches an internal temperature of 135°F/57°C, about 15 minutes. **REMOVE** it to a cutting board or plate while you make the sauce.

- **PUT** the roasting skillet over medium heat, **ADD** 1 tablespoon olive oil, and **SAUTÉ** the garlic till tender, about a minute. **HOLD** a strainer over the pan and **DUMP** the tomatoes into the strainer so that the tomato water drains into the pan. **SET** the strainer with the tomatoes back in the bowl. When the tomato water simmers, **WHISK** or **STIR** in the butter, one piece at a time, keeping the liquid moving until all of the butter is melted. **ADD** the tomatoes and any additional liquid in the bowl. **ADD** the basil and **STIR**.

- **SERVE** the fish sliced into thick medallions on a bed of tomatoes and garnished with extra basil.

SMOKE-ROASTED JERKED
CORNISH HENS

SMOKE ROASTING, LIKE SPIT ROASTING, IS A METHOD CLOSELY aligned with the original definition of roasting—cooking meat with actual flames and coals. And it serves to underscore the reason that roasted meats were traditionally considered superior to meats cooked in an oven: because they are indeed more delicious, having picked up the complex aromas that smoke imparts to meats. Smoke roasting, likewise, yields flavors and succulence that can't be achieved any other way.

Smoke roasting is distinguished from true smoking by the high temperature. We smoke meat at temperatures below those at which food browns, such as bacon, though a side of bacon nevertheless cooks at 200°F/95°C. Furthermore, with smoking, we introduce wood smoke to the cooking enclosure. With smoke roasting, we cook primarily over indirect high heat, 300°F/150°C or higher, with smoke generated by the dripping fat

Try this butter spiked with jerk paste for an excellent variation on a traditional roasted chicken.

and coals. Wood can be added to the fire for additional smoke flavor, but what distinguishes smoke roasting is that the meat is cooked in an enclosure with live coals and high heat.

Any of the meats in this book can be smoke roasted rather than oven roasted. Think of it as simply turning your charcoal grill into an oven. A hot fire in a kettle grill will create an oven temperature of 350°F/180°C to 500°F/260°C. Japanese kamado grills, egg-shaped coal-fueled ovens, originally earthenware but now made of thick ceramics, can reach temperatures of 800°F/425°C and are likewise excellent for smoke roasting. Sorry, all you folks with gas grills—smoke roasting involves indirect heat, and gas grills allow too much heat to escape to smoke roast with any kind of efficiency or consistency. Your best bet is to cook directly over gas flames to sear the meat and pick up some smoke, and then finish the birds in a 350°F/180°C oven.

The basic technique requires cooking the meat for a short time over high direct heat to begin the browning process, which creates rich, complex flavors. Once you've got a good sear on the meat, move it to the cooler half of the grill and then cover the grill, leaving the vents open to maintain the heat of the coals.

Here, I employ the technique on Cornish hens, seasoned with jerk paste. I love the flavors of jerk, the Jamaican blend of chiles, allspice, and other pungent spices. Jerk paste is available at most grocery stores these days, but I encourage you to try making your own (the chef and writer David Tanis offered an excellent version in the May 3, 2013, issue of the *New York Times;* I highly recommend it). Traditional jerk is always cooked over live coals; I'm sure it's no coincidence that the seasoning blends particularly well with the flavors of smoke.

To enhance the succulence of the jerked poultry, which can lack moisture given the high, dry heat, I not only rub the poultry with jerk paste, I also make a jerk-butter baste. This is very nontraditional where jerk is concerned, but it adds the richness of butter, and the butter solids brown on the skin, adding even more flavor. I like to serve this with a colorful black bean salad (see page 52) for a cool summer meal, or you could pair it with yellow rice and beans or whatever you wish. The smoke-roasted bird is the focal point of the meal.

2 Cornish hens

Kosher salt

2 tablespoons jerk paste, or to taste

Juice of ½ lime

6 tablespoons/90 grams cold butter,

cut into 4 or 5 pieces

SERVES 2 TO 4

- **SPATCHCOCK** the birds—that is, **REMOVE** their backbones so that you can flatten them out. (This isn't difficult to do, but you can ask your butcher or grocery store meat department to do it for you if you wish.) **HOLD** the bird, neck side down, on the cutting board, with the spine toward you and its butt end (Pope's nose) up and toward you. **RUN** a sharp knife down either side of the backbone, cutting through the rib bones to completely separate it from the rest of the bird (this can also be done with kitchen shears if you prefer). **SAVE** the backbone for stock. **CUT** off the wing tips and **SAVE** these as well. **TURN** the bird over and **SPREAD** out the rib cage, with the legs facing up, by pressing down on the breast. **TIE** the ends of the drumsticks together if you wish; it makes flipping the birds easier.

- **GIVE** both sides a liberal salting and **ALLOW** the salt to dissolve and begin to penetrate the meat for at least 10 minutes, or up to 2 days in advance of applying the jerk paste.

- **PREPARE** a fire that has enough coals to cover the area below half of the grill.

- **RUB** each hen with the jerk paste—2 teaspoons (or more) if you like it fiery, 1 teaspoon if you prefer a milder spiciness.

- When the coals are vivid orange and ashy, **SPREAD** them out to cover half of the bottom of the grill, and **PUT** the grill rack in place. **ALLOW** the rack to get hot, a good 5 minutes or so.

- **PUT** the lime juice in a small saucepan over high heat. Once the pan begins to get hot, 5 or 10 seconds, **ADD** a chunk of butter to the pan and **SWIRL** it till it begins to melt. **ADD** the remaining butter, piece by piece, and keep swirling until all of the butter is completely melted, a minute or two. **REMOVE** the pan from the heat and **SWIRL** in 1 tablespoon jerk paste.

- **PLACE** the hens, skin side down, directly over the coals and **GRILL** until they are beautifully seared and browned, 5 to 10 minutes depending on your fire. **FLIP** the birds, **MOVE** them to the cool side of the grill, and **COVER** the grill. After 10 minutes of smoke roasting, **FLIP** the birds again and **BASTE** the underside with the jerk butter. **COVER** and **ROAST** for 10 minutes. **FLIP** them again and **BASTE** with the remaining butter. **COVER** and continue roasting. **REMOVE** the birds when they're cooked, after 40 to 50 minutes of total cooking time.

- **ALLOW** the birds to rest for 10 minutes before serving. **SERVE** one hen per person for dinner or, for four smaller portions, **HALVE** the birds lengthwise through the center of the breastbone.

THE FINER POINTS

SALT

Salt the birds far enough in advance that it has a chance to penetrate the skin and meat. Because salt is a powerful antibacterial agent and flavor enhancer, it's best to salt the meat the day before smoke roasting and refrigerate it, uncovered. As an added bonus, salt also helps dehydrate the skin so that it crisps up nicely.

BASTING

For the baste, I use what is basically a *beurre blanc* technique. Butter is emulsified into a liquid (flavorful lime juice here) so that it remains homogenized rather than separated, to facilitate even distribution when basting. (This lime butter is a great all-purpose baste base—add Dijon mustard, minced shallot, and chopped fresh tarragon for an excellent variation.)

JERK CHICKEN

Feel free to use this method with a whole spatchcocked chicken (it will take about 1 hour total cooking time, depending on its size). Or use a cut-up chicken—drumsticks and thighs work best with the jerk seasoning and cooking method, but bone-in, skin-on breasts will turn out fine as well.

SPIT-ROASTED
LEG OF LAMB

THIS IS THE ORIGINAL FORM OF ROASTING, MEAT TURNING ON a spit, licked by flames, caressed by drifting smoke. There's a reason it's one of the most compelling visions in cooking, why people will stop and stare, mesmerized by the sight of it. It was how *Homo sapiens* cooked meat for two hundred thousand years (if not longer), and some have argued that it contributed to the evolution of our current selves, big-brained storytellers, the only animal that cooks food.

Spit roasting is the perfect way to cook large, tough cuts of meat, such as a big pork shoulder or, here, a bone-in leg of lamb. All you need is a spit and a place to burn wood or coal. Or, of course, a grill that comes with a rotisserie. But stand-alone rotisseries are inexpensive, and there's no reason you couldn't improvise a fire pit out back or set one up in front of any decent-sized fireplace. Whole hogs are often spit roasted over a low coal fire but, for the most part, spit roasting is accomplished using indirect heat, with the fire and coals beside the turning meat, and a drip pan directly below it.

I'm lucky enough to have a wife and colleague who designed a big fire pit for a side patio at our suburban castle, and I was able to buy a spit, with a rotisserie motor, just long enough to stretch from one edge to the other. I've found spit roasting to be such a pleasure that I can foresee bringing the practice indoors for festive winter parties. Not only is the resulting meat delicious, but a large part of the enjoyment is being able to watch it cooking, as the skin turns gradually to crisp, golden brown, with the fat frothing out of the skin and sliding over the surface as the meat turns.

The flavors of flame and smoke pair beautifully with lamb. How you want to embellish the meat is up to you and, really, secondary to this excellent and ancient roasting technique. I urge you to improvise with your own seasonings, relying on what you like and what goes well with lamb. Lots of black pepper is always a good idea and, as with beef, cracked coriander seed is excellent with lamb. And I don't think I'd ever omit garlic when cooking lamb. You can make it spicy, with cumin and ancho chiles; you can take it in a curry direction, with curry and chili powders or the Moroccan spice *ras el hanout;* or you can keep it traditional, with herbs and even more garlic.

For this recipe, I salted the meat a day before cooking it, studded it with sliced garlic cloves (many of which squeezed out, horn-like, as the meat cooked and the protein contracted), and then coated it with black pepper. I cooked plenty of garlic and a bunch of fresh oregano in a cup of olive oil with which to baste the slowly turning meat, and gave it a delicate sprinkling of chopped fresh rosemary at the end. I served the lamb with roasted potatoes, roasted green beans, and a *chimichurri* sauce, a basic vinaigrette loaded with chopped fresh oregano, parsley, and chives.

A bone-in leg of lamb usually comes with part of the pelvis still attached to the leg bone. The lamb will be easier to carve if you remove this part before putting the lamb on the spit. You can ask your butcher to do it or simply work your knife around the bone, wiggling it to get a sense of where the ball joint is, and then cut through the ligaments holding the joint together.

I chose to cook a bone-in leg, but spit roasting works fine with a boneless leg. Simply tie it tightly using slipknots (see page 45)—you could spread the interior with coarse-grained mustard, garlic, and fresh herbs first—or ask your butcher to tie it for you. A general rule of thumb is that it will take about 15 minutes per pound to cook, but this depends on how hot you keep your fire, the ambient temperature, and how long you've let it sit at room temperature before cooking. You'll want to rely on a thermometer to gauge when the meat is done.

1 (8- to 10-pound/3.5- to 4.5-kilogram) bone-in leg of lamb

Kosher salt

10 garlic cloves

1 cup/240 milliliters olive oil

1 bunch fresh oregano

Freshly ground black pepper

SERVES 8 TO 10

- The day before cooking, **COVER** the leg with a uniform layer of kosher salt and refrigerate it, uncovered. **REMOVE** it from the refrigerator 4 to 6 hours before you're ready to start cooking and **LET** it sit at room temperature.

- **TIE** the lamb with 4 or 5 lengths of butcher's string. **THRUST** your spit through the center of the meat, as close to the bones as possible, and **PRESS** the rotisserie forks into the meat to secure it.

- **CUT** half of the garlic cloves into thick wedges and use a paring knife to **SLIDE** them into the muscle all over the leg. **POUR** the olive oil into a small saucepan. Lightly **SMASH** the remaining garlic cloves and **ADD** them to the oil, along with the oregano, and **WARM** gently over medium heat to infuse the oil. **ALLOW** it to cool a bit and **RUB** some of the warm oil on the meat and then **DUST** the meat generously with freshly ground black pepper.

- **PREPARE** your fire so that you have plenty of hot coals and, behind them, flaming logs becoming embers. **SET** the rotisserie as close to the fire as you can. **PUT** your hand in front of the meat—it should be too hot to hold your hand there for long. If it's not that hot, **PUT** more wood on the fire. **PLACE** a foil drip pan below the meat.

- **COOK** the lamb, basting it frequently with the oil, until a thermometer reaches 120°F to 125°F/49°C to 52°C at the thickest part of the leg, about 15 minutes per pound.

- **ALLOW** the meat to rest for at least 30 minutes and up to 1 hour before slicing.

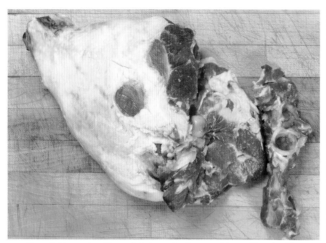

Step 1. Removing the pelvic bone before cooking will make the lamb easier to carve.

Step 2. Baste frequently as the leg of lamb cooks over the open flames.

Step 3. When the lamb reaches an internal temperature of 120° to 125°F/49° to 52°C (for rare), it's time to remove it from the spit.

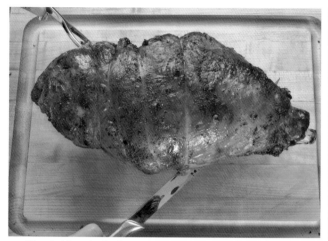

Step 4. Allow the lamb to rest for a minimum of 30 minutes, and as long as an hour, before carving.

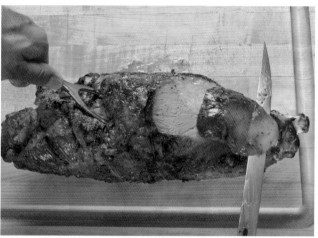

Step 5. To carve, secure the leg on its side.

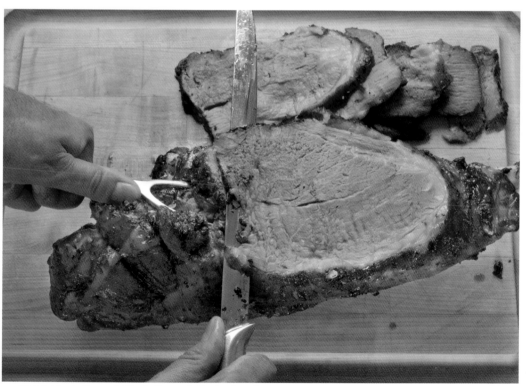

Step 6. Carve slices with the knife parallel to the board.

BROCCOLI
WITH GARLIC

I LOVE PERFECTLY COOKED BROCCOLI, THE STEMS TENDER
but still with some bite, served piping hot with butter and lemon juice and
salt. In my experience, however, you have to be extremely conscientious to prepare and serve boiled or steamed broccoli well. The window between crunchy
and mushy is small, and with all that surface area, the vegetable gets lukewarm
fast. Mushy, lukewarm broccoli just doesn't taste good.

Roasted broccoli is the best broccoli, in my opinion. Properly done, the
broccoli gets partly browned, producing a more complex flavor, and some of
the florets get crispy to offset the softness.
And it's not difficult—anyone over the age
of seven who has hands should be able
produce superlative roasted broccoli every
time. (Of course, most green vegetables are
delicious roasted; two of my other favorites

Because green vegetables
have so much moisture in
them, always roast at high
heat and use convection
if you have it.

are green beans, with red pepper flakes, cumin, and garlic, and asparagus, with just salt and lemon zest to finish.)

Broccoli, like all green vegetables, is composed largely of water, so high heat is required. In order to conduct the heat to this moist vegetable, it helps to coat the broccoli with oil. Finally, we can add some additional flavor in the form of whole garlic cloves, which brown and take on a mild, nutty sweetness while they season the oil. Extra credit goes to those who trim the green fibrous exterior from the thick parts of the main stem and cut the sweet, tender white interior into chunks (to eat as is, or to roast along with the rest of the broccoli).

The second of the two keys to perfectly roasted broccoli, after giving the vegetable a uniform coating of oil, is choosing the right cooking vessel. You need a large enough area for the florets to spread out; if they're bunched up, they'll steam and won't brown. But spread them out too much and they may burn. So choose a surface that allows you to spread them in a single, comfortable layer. The vessel should also have low sides so that there's plenty of circulation to sweep the released moisture away from the broccoli and facilitate browning and even cooking. Circulation is critical to roasting most vegetables, and especially broccoli, so choosing the wrong pan can doom you from the start. And, because circulation is so important, use convection heat if you have it.

Florets from 2 heads broccoli

6 or 7 fat garlic cloves

3 tablespoons olive oil

Kosher salt

4 lemon wedges (optional)

SERVES 4

- **PREHEAT** the oven to 425°F/220°C (use convection if you have it).

- **COMBINE** the broccoli florets and garlic in a large bowl. **DRIZZLE** half of the olive oil over them and **GIVE** them a thorough tossing. **DRIZZLE** on the remaining oil and **TOSS** some more. **ADD** an aggressive four-finger pinch of salt as you toss.

- When the broccoli and garlic are uniformly coated with the oil, **DUMP** them into a large ovenproof sauté pan. **ROAST** for 15 minutes. **REMOVE** the pan and **TOSS** the broccoli, and then continue roasting until some of the florets are brown and crispy and the stems are al dente, 5 to 10 minutes more.

- **SERVE** immediately, with lemon wedges for seasoning, or **KEEP** the broccoli warm in the hot pan (out of the oven) if you need time to get other dishes on the table.

THE BEST WAY TO COOK
BRUSSELS SPROUTS

WANT YOUR KID TO EAT BRUSSELS SPROUTS? ROAST THEM!

And how often do you hear your spouse crowing over how delicious the Brussels sprouts are?

It's the power of roast: high heat and the complex flavors it creates.

The method follows the same basic rationale as for broccoli, but the Brussels sprout is a dense vegetable with relatively little surface area. So, while you can roast whole Brussels sprouts with fine results, I like to halve or quarter them—more surface area means more browning, and therefore more flavor. (The downside is that you lose a lot of exterior leaves, so if you're short on sprouts, roast them whole, giving them about 15 more minutes till they're tender. And by tender I mean that when you insert a paring knife into one, the sprout offers no resistance.)

These are fabulous cooked with bacon fat and bacon, my favorite way to roast them. Or they can be finished with a little olive oil or butter, salt, and pepper, which is how I typically serve them. But if you want to take the dish to another level, dress them with a nutty vinaigrette. In his book *Live to Cook*, my

friend and colleague Michael Symon included a fantastic recipe for deep-fried Brussels sprouts tossed with a walnut vinaigrette. If you want to try this, combine 1 tablespoon minced shallots with 2 tablespoons good red wine vinegar, add a pinch of kosher salt and let it sit for a few minutes, and stir in ¼ cup/60 milliliters walnut or vegetable oil and some toasted chopped walnuts. Even easier, you could simply sprinkle the roasted sprouts with a bit of red wine vinegar just before serving—a pungent vegetable benefits from the acidity.

The same rules for broccoli apply here. Apply a uniform coating of oil, which conducts the heat; choose a low-sided pan that won't discourage circulation, sized so that the sprouts fit in a single snug layer; use high heat, and convection if you have it. And, like broccoli, Brussels sprouts will stay delicious even if you finish them early; simply return them to the oven 5 minutes before you want to serve them.

1 pound Brussels sprouts

¼ cup/60 milliliters vegetable oil

Kosher salt

SERVES 4

- **PREHEAT** the oven to 425°F/220°C (use convection if you have it).

- **TRIM** the root end of each Brussels sprout but **LEAVE** enough of the root to hold the leaves on it. **HALVE** or **QUARTER** the sprouts (if they're tiny, halve them; otherwise I prefer quartered—more surface area).

- In a large bowl, **TOSS** the sprouts with the oil and 2 large pinches of salt. **DUMP** them into a heavy ovenproof sauté pan and **ROAST**, stirring and tossing once or twice, till they are nicely browned and tender, 30 to 45 minutes. **SERVE** immediately or **KEEP** the sprouts warm in the hot pan until ready to serve.

CAULI-FLOWER
THREE WAYS

I'VE WRITTEN ABOUT THIS BEFORE BUT I HAVE TO INCLUDE it again here, with a couple of variations, because the transformation from crunchy raw veg to exquisite, complex, nutty deliciousness is so dramatic. I merely mention it aloud and the thought makes Donna exclaim, "Oh! So good!"

It really is as simple as high heat, a skillet, and plenty of butter. High heat to caramelize the big, moist vegetable; a skillet to encourage circulation (I use cast iron); and butter to help cook it (the butter also browns with the cauliflower, adding that wonderfully complex browned-butter flavor).

I'll describe the basic recipe first, and then go into the variations. I like to roast a whole head of cauliflower because it's a beautiful centerpiece for a family-style meal. But it takes a good hour to cook, so when I forget to get it into the oven in time, I cut the cauliflower into florets and roast them as I would broccoli.

When you're pan roasting it's best to use a side towel, rather than an awkward potholder, to retrieve the pan; leave that towel on the pan's handle anytime it's out of the oven so no one mistakenly grabs it and gets burned.

Basic Roasted Cauliflower

1 head cauliflower

6 tablespoons/90 grams butter, at room temperature

Kosher salt

SERVES 4

- **PREHEAT** the oven to 425°F/220°C (use convection if you have it).

- **CUT** the stem and leaves off the cauliflower so that it will sit flat in a skillet; the more of the cauliflower that's in contact with the skillet the better, as it gets very brown and tasty.

- **SET** the cauliflower in an ovenproof skillet and **SMEAR** the butter all over the surface. **GIVE** it a liberal sprinkling of salt.

- **ROAST** till tender (a long knife should slide easily down into the cauliflower all the way through to its stem), 1 hour to 1 hour 15 minutes. Several times while it's roasting, **BASTE** it with the butter, which will have melted and started to brown. (If you're roasting a cut-up cauliflower, simply **PUT** the florets and butter in the skillet and **PUT** it in the oven. After 5 or 10 minutes, **STIR** and **TOSS** the cauliflower to coat the florets with the melted butter, and then continue roasting and basting till tender, 30 to 40 minutes.)

- **SERVE** immediately, in wedges or slices, or **KEEP** warm and **REHEAT** for a few minutes in a hot oven before serving.

Roasted Cauliflower
with Capers, Anchovies, Raisins, and Pine Nuts

2 anchovies, minced

2 tablespoons capers, coarsely chopped

2 tablespoons golden raisins, coarsely chopped

1 tablespoon balsamic vinegar

1 head cauliflower, cut into florets and roasted

¼ cup/40 grams toasted pine nuts

1 tablespoon minced fresh parsley

SERVES 4

- In a small bowl, **COMBINE** the anchovies, capers, raisins, and balsamic vinegar and **STIR** to combine. **SPRINKLE** the mixture over the cauliflower and **STIR** to distribute the garnish uniformly. **SPRINKLE** the pine nuts over the cauliflower, followed by the parsley, and **SERVE** right from the skillet.

Step 1. Smear or pour soft butter all over the cauliflower and roast.

Step 2. Baste frequently during the hourlong cook.

Step 3. The quirky cauliflower Polonaise with its garnishes.

Step 4. A whole roasted cauliflower garnished with hard-cooked egg, bread crumbs, and parsley makes a great centerpiece for a meat-free meal or an impressive side dish for roasted meat or fish.

Roasted Cauliflower Polonaise

Boiled cauliflower with hard-cooked eggs, bread crumbs, and parsley? When I first learned this old preparation, in a culinary basics class at the CIA, I thought it was too goofy for words. But when I asked my cooking partner, Adam Shepard, what he thought of it, he said, "I'd serve it at my restaurant. Though I'd figure out a way to make the egg and bread crumbs stick to the cauliflower." That he took it seriously made me take it seriously. As my appreciation of classic dishes grew, so too did my affection for this dish. Prepare it with roasted cauliflower rather than boiled, and it becomes a great dish for any occasion.

1 head cauliflower (whole or cut into florets), roasted

1 tablespoon butter, if needed

¼ cup/20 grams panko bread crumbs

1 lemon wedge

1 or 2 hard-cooked eggs, chopped

3 tablespoons chopped fresh parsley

SERVES 4

- **PLACE** the hot roasted cauliflower on a serving platter. If there is no remaining butter in the skillet, **ADD** another tablespoon. **ADD** the bread crumbs to the skillet and **COOK** over medium-high heat till they're toasted.

- **SQUEEZE** the lemon over the cauliflower and then **SPOON** the toasted bread crumbs over the cauliflower. **SPOON** the chopped egg over the cauliflower (don't worry if it doesn't stick). **SPRINKLE** it with parsley and **SERVE** in wedges or slices, scooping up extra garnish as you do so.

- If you're using roasted florets, **MELT** 1 tablespoon butter in a separate small skillet over medium-high heat and **TOAST** the bread crumbs. To serve, simply **SPRINKLE** the lemon juice, toasted bread crumbs, chopped egg, and parsley uniformly over the top of the florets and **SERVE** right from the skillet.

ROASTED
RED
PEPPERS

ADDING ROASTED RED PEPPERS to your culinary repertoire is a game changer. What begins as a crunchy, mildly flavorful, juicy vegetable (fruit, technically) becomes a sweetly aromatic ingredient in pasta, rice, salad, or soup. Indeed, there's almost no dish that isn't improved with the addition of roasted red peppers. They're easy to make and all but impossible to screw up. And, finally, my favorite element, the name: they are truly roasted—that is, cooked over fire. I roast them over a direct flame on my gas burner, the sweet charred aroma from the burning skin filling the kitchen. (They can be broiled if you don't have a gas range. It's not roasting, but the effect is nearly the same.)

The idea is simple. Char the exterior of the pepper till it's completely black, and then let the pepper cool in an enclosed environment (I use a brown paper bag) so that the charred skin separates from the sweet flesh. But how they are transformed into such a versatile, sweet-smoky seasoning mystifies.

1 red bell pepper

- If you have a gas range, **PUT** the pepper on the grate directly over high flames until it's fully charred on the side facing the flames. Use tongs to **TURN** the pepper and continue to **COOK** until all surfaces are charred, bottom and top as well. (Undercharred skin can be difficult to remove.)

- When the pepper is completely charred, **PUT** it in a paper bag and **CLOSE** it up tight, or **PUT** it in a bowl and **COVER** securely with plastic wrap.

- When the pepper is cool, **RUB** off the skin under cold running water. **PULL** the flesh away from the stem, **TEAR** or **SLICE** in half, **RINSE** away any seeds, and **PULL** off any white ribs that remain inside.

- The red pepper is ready to use at this point or you can refrigerate it, covered, for up to 3 days.

- If you don't have a gas range, you can broil the pepper with virtually identical results. **PREHEAT** the broiler. **SLICE** the pepper in half lengthwise and **REMOVE** the seeds and ribs. **PUT** the halves on a baking sheet, cut sides down, and **SET** them under the broiler until they are thoroughly charred, about 20 minutes, depending on the strength of your broiler.

DUCK FAT–ROASTED POTATOES WITH ONION AND ROSEMARY

OF ALL THE VEGETABLES WE ROAST, potatoes are probably the most common, and for good reason. Inexpensive, easy to prepare, and delicious as a side dish, roasted potatoes deserve to be a regular feature of your dinner table. Of course, potatoes are good cooked in any neutral oil, but cook them in animal fat and they take on a crispness and richness that vegetable oils can't replicate. Here I recommend duck fat, but you can also use rendered chicken fat (schmaltz), pork fat, or even beef fat.

As with all vegetables, you want to use high heat for potatoes. With this recipe I introduce the very moist onion to the mix, which adds great flavor but can also diminish crispness. To prevent this from happening, it's important to get the timing right.

Roasting potatoes in animal fat (as opposed to vegetable oil) enhances their flavor and makes them especially crispy.

The potatoes need twice as much time in the high heat, so I don't add the onions until halfway through the roasting time. I salt at this stage as well, but I don't add the final seasoning, rosemary, until the piping-hot potatoes come out of the oven—this maximizes the release of the herb's volatile oils.

¼ cup/60 milliliters duck fat

2 large russet potatoes, peeled and cut into medium dice

½ large Spanish onion, cut into medium dice

Kosher salt

Freshly ground black pepper

1 tablespoon minced fresh rosemary

SERVES 4

- **PUT** a roasting pan (preferably nonstick) or baking sheet in the oven and **PREHEAT** it to 425°F/220°C (use convection if you have it).

- When the oven and roasting pan are hot, **PUT** the fat in the pan (allowing it to melt if it's cold) and **ADD** the potatoes, stirring immediately so that they all get coated with fat. **ALLOW** the potatoes to roast untouched for 30 minutes. **REMOVE** the pan from the oven and **STIR** the potatoes, scraping up any that have stuck to the pan. **ADD** the onion and 2 four-finger pinches of salt and **STIR** again to distribute the onion and salt evenly. Continue roasting until the potatoes are golden brown and crispy, 20 to 30 minutes.

- **REMOVE** the potatoes from the oven and **GRIND** pepper generously over them. **SPRINKLE** the rosemary over them, **STIR** to distribute, and **SERVE** immediately.

THE FINER POINTS

You can peel and dice the potatoes and store them in a bowl of water in the refrigerator for up to 3 days before cooking. Drain them well and pat them dry before adding them to the pan. (The more water they have on them, the more they'll cool down the roasting pan when you add them. The water will also cool the fat and increase the likelihood of the potatoes' sticking, so the drier they are, the better.)

Many grocery stores carry rendered chicken and duck fat. Duck fat is also readily available online from many sources, but I encourage you to roast a duck, saving excess fat and rendering it yourself by cooking it over a low flame till the fat liquefies. Other fats can be used as well— fat from rendered bacon, the fat rendered when you roast a chicken. That's flavor—don't throw it out!

Don't go by time alone when roasting potatoes. They're done when they look delicious to eat, and you know when that is. If you think they'll be done before the rest of the meal, pull them from the oven just before they are done, then return them to the oven 5 to 10 minutes before you need them.

ROASTED
ROOT VEGE- TABLES

ROASTING A VARIETY OF ROOT VEGETABLES IS AN ESPECIALLY nutritious way to offer diverse, complex flavors. The star here is the beet, which not only adds great flavor and sweetness but also gives otherwise drab vegetables a dynamic and inviting hue. The method follows the same mandates as for roasted potatoes: high heat, animal fat (here, from bacon) for crispness and flavor, and the moist onion added midway through cooking. Vegetable or olive oil can replace the bacon fat if you wish, but I appreciate the way the smoky cured flavor of bacon brings all the flavors together. I prefer lardons, thick batons of bacon I cut from slab bacon; thick-cut bacon is fine if that's all that's available to you. Finally, all this starch and sweetness benefits from a bit of acid, so I finish with a sprinkling of red wine vinegar (and some more fat—this time, olive oil).

¼ pound/110 grams bacon lardons or thick-cut bacon, cut into strips

2 parsnips, peeled and cut into bite-size pieces

3 small red beets, peeled and cut into bite-size pieces

1 celery root, peeled and cut into bite-size pieces

2 Yukon Gold potatoes, peeled and cut into bite-size pieces

2 carrots, peeled and cut into bite-size pieces

1 Spanish onion, cut into large dice

5 to 10 garlic cloves, halved

Kosher salt

Freshly ground black pepper

2 teaspoons red wine vinegar

1 tablespoon extra-virgin olive oil

SERVES 6

- **PREHEAT** the oven to 425°F/220°C (or 450°F/230°C if your oven is clean; use convection at either temperature if you have it).

- **COOK** the bacon over medium heat on the stovetop until the fat has rendered and the bacon is tender, about 15 minutes (this can be done in a skillet or directly in the roasting pan you will use for the vegetables).

- **COMBINE** the bacon and rendered fat with the parsnips, beets, celery root, potatoes, and carrots in a roasting pan, stirring well to coat the vegetables in fat. **ROAST** for 20 minutes. **ADD** the onion, garlic, and 2 or 3 generous pinches of salt to the pan and **STIR** to distribute the onion and garlic. Continue to **COOK** until the vegetables are browned and tender, another 40 minutes or so, stirring again if you wish.

- **REMOVE** the pan from the oven and **GIVE** the vegetables a generous grinding of black pepper. **SPRINKLE** the vinegar over the top, followed by the olive oil. **TOSS** and then **SERVE** immediately.

Step 1. Bacon is partially rendered.

Step 2. Bacon and bacon fat are a great flavoring and enriching device for starchy root vegetables.

Step 3. Beets are a critical component to these roasted vegetables, for both their color and their sweetness.

Step 4. Finish the dish with more salt to taste, vinegar, and olive oil.

ROASTED TOMATO SAUCE AND A HABANERO SALSA VARIATION

ROASTING TOMATOES IS A QUICK AND EASY WAY TO MAKE FRESH, delicious tomato sauce. The high heat partially dehydrates the tomatoes and their skin becomes charred, enhancing the flavor.

This recipe produces an all-purpose tomato sauce for homemade pizza, pasta, or grilled chicken, or you can use it as the base for any number of more complex sauces. Press it through a fine-mesh strainer and add cream for a rich, smoky tomato soup. Roast some onion or garlic along with the tomatoes and add them to the blender. Use butter rather than olive oil. Add a tablespoon of minced fresh oregano. Any of these variations will give you a slightly different flavor, but the basic method is the same. I also include instructions here for turning the roasted tomatoes into a habanero salsa for chips.

No tomato sauce in a jar can match a sauce you make from fresh tomatoes; it's simple and delicious— and it saves money.

10 Roma tomatoes, halved lengthwise

¼ to ⅓ cup/60 to 80 milliliters olive oil

½ teaspoon kosher salt

MAKES 3 TO 4 CUPS/700 TO 950 MILLILITERS

- **PREHEAT** the oven to 450°F/230°C (or 425°F/220°C if you have convection); if your oven has not been cleaned in a while, use 425°F/220°C (400°F/200°C convection).

- **SPREAD** out the tomatoes on a baking sheet, cut sides down. **ROAST** until well charred, 30 to 40 minutes (they can't be too charred). **PUREE** them in a blender with the olive oil and salt (be sure to leave the blender top open and cover it with a towel to prevent the lid from blowing off). **USE** immediately or **COOL** and **STORE** in the refrigerator for up to 5 days or in the freezer for up to 3 months.

- To make roasted tomato-habanero salsa, simply **ADD** 4 habanero chiles and 6 peeled garlic cloves to the baking sheet and **ROAST** them with the tomatoes. When the chiles are cool enough to handle, **PULL** off the stems and **SHAKE** out any seeds. **PUREE** the tomatoes, chiles, garlic, and salt until smooth. I don't add olive oil or other fat to this. **SERVE** chilled or at room temperature.

BROWN
VEAL
STOCK

ROASTED VEAL STOCK IS SUCH an extraordinary substance that I've been writing about it for more than a decade and never tire of trumpeting its wonders. I include it here because it is the purest expression of roasting. It is roasting distilled, the very essence of roasting.

Veal stock is considered a "neutral" stock—especially "white" (non-roasted) veal stock. Veal stock tends to play up and enhance other flavors. For instance, if you add it to chicken stock and reduce the mixture for a sauce, miraculously the sauce tastes more intensely of chicken. Because of this neutrality, veal stock itself also highlights the flavors of roasting, the complex flavors achieved when meat protein and bone are cooked at high temperatures.

But just because it's neutral doesn't mean it's insipid. On the contrary, it's extraordinarily rich and has great body. Veal bones, bones of young animals, are loaded with collagen, the protein that composes the connective tissue of joints and tendons;

If there's one preparation that can elevate home cooking to the level of the food in a great restaurant, it's veal stock.

collagen breaks down in cooking to create gelatin, the stuff that gives a stock body. Reduced veal stock should set up so solidly you can bounce it on a counter.

The meat on the bones gives the stock its characteristic flavor, and the vegetables and aromatics complete the stock.

Depending on where you live, veal bones can be hard to find. You should be able to order them from the meat department at your grocery store or butcher, or request them at your farmers' market. Alternatively, you can simply buy a whole, bone-in veal breast, which has a great ratio of bone, cartilage, and meat. The bones are usually soft enough to cut and chop through with a knife so that they can be made into many pieces, thus increasing the surface area, and thus increasing the amount of browning flavor you can get into your stock. It's not hard to do, but you can ask your butcher to do it for you instead.

Roasted veal stock follows all the customary rules of stock making. Bones and meat are cooked in water that is hot but not bubbling—185°F/85°C is optimal. Vegetables and other aromatics are added during the last hour or so. The stock is strained through cloth, and the fat is removed from the surface. The main difference is that the cooking time is considerably longer than it is for chicken stock—10 to 12 hours, ideally. And even with all that cooking, the bones will still have flavor in them, so many restaurant kitchens recook the bones to make a second stock, called a *rémouillage,* which they add to the first stock, a technique that's worth the effort as it can increase the yield by up to 30 percent.

The following is a recipe for a basic brown veal stock. Traditionally, the vegetables are browned, which adds a deeper color and flavor to the stock, but it's a step I usually don't trouble with; I find the stock is complex enough without caramelizing the vegetables.

1 (4-pound/1.8-kilogram) veal breast or

4 pounds/1.8 kilograms meaty, cartilaginous veal bones

3 large carrots, cut into large dice

1 large Spanish onion, cut into large dice

(if the papery brown skin is clean, include this as well)

5 to 10 garlic cloves

¼ cup/60 grams tomato paste

2 teaspoons black peppercorns,

lightly crushed in a mortar or beneath a sauté pan

3 bay leaves

MAKES 2.5 QUARTS/LITERS

- **PREHEAT** the oven to 425°F/220°C (use convection if you have it).

- **CUT** the veal breast into 2- by 3-inch/5- by 7.5-centimeter pieces. On a baking sheet, **ARRANGE** the pieces so that there's plenty of space between them to allow for good circulation. **ROAST** them until they are golden brown and look like they'd be delicious to eat (and they would be), 30 to 45 minutes. **REDUCE** the oven temperature to 200°F/95°C (without convection).

- **CHOOSE** a pot that will hold the meat and bones snugly in two layers and **COVER** with about 4 inches/10 centimeters of water. **PLACE** the pot, uncovered, in the oven for 10 to 12 hours. If possible, **CHECK** the water level midway through the cooking to ensure that the bones are covered. If they aren't, **ADD** more water.

- **REMOVE** the pot from the oven. **ADD** more water to cover the bones by a couple of inches if it has cooked down. **ADD** the carrots, onion, and garlic (**SAUTÉ** the vegetables until caramelized first, if you wish, adding the tomato paste toward the end and cooking that as well), along with the remaining ingredients. **ADD** more water as necessary. **BRING** the pot just to a simmer over high heat, **REDUCE** the heat to low (the pot should be too hot to touch, but the water should not be bubbling), and **COOK** for 1 hour.

- **STRAIN** the stock through a colander, basket strainer, or *chinois*. (If you intend to make a *rémouillage*, **DISCARD** the vegetables and **PUT** the bones back in the pot, **COVER** them with water, and **COOK** them again in a 200°F/95°C oven or over low heat on top of the stove for 6 hours, and **ADD** this to your stock. **STRAIN** the stock again through cloth.)

- **CHILL** the veal stock completely and **LIFT** the fat off the surface. The stock will keep refrigerated up to 1 week or frozen up to 3 months.

What to Do with Veal Stock

- Needless to say, veal stock makes a great sauce for veal. **SAUTÉ** veal scaloppini in olive oil or butter and **REMOVE** them from the pan; **ADD** 2 tablespoons minced shallots and **COOK**. **DEGLAZE** with ½ cup/120 milliliters dry white wine and **REDUCE** by half; **ADD** 1 cup/240 milliliters veal stock and **REDUCE** by half, whisking in 2 tablespoons/30 grams butter as you do.
- For a classic veal stew, **SIMMER** diced veal shoulder or stewing meat in the veal stock, **THICKEN** the sauce (**KNEAD** 1 tablespoon flour into 1 tablespoon room-temperature butter and **WHISK** this into the sauce), and then **ADD** ½ cup/120 milliliters cream mixed with an egg yolk. **ADD** sautéed mushrooms and pearl onions at the end and **SERVE** over egg noodles. (Add Dijon mustard to this same sauce and it's fabulous with pork.)
- **ADD** 1 cup/240 milliliters veal stock to roasted chicken *jus* for an over-the-top chicken gravy.
- **ENRICH** any braise or stew with 1 cup/240 milliliters veal stock.

Step 1. A bone-in veal breast is the perfect cut for making roasted veal stock, one of the magical ingredients of the kitchen.

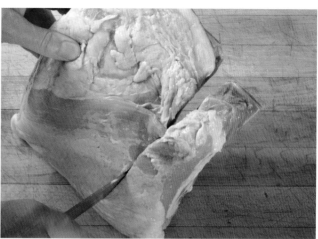

Step 2. Slice through the bone and cartilage where you find natural seams.

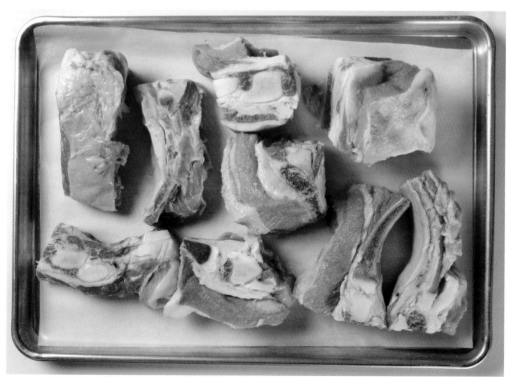

Step 3. Cut the veal into pieces to increase surface area.

Step 4. More browned surface results in more roasted flavor.

Step 5. Roasted veal bones are held in hot but not bubbling water, 185° to 190°F/85° to 88°C, for 10 to 12 hours.

Step 6. Aromatic herbs and vegetables are added at the end of the cooking for flavor and sweetness.

Step 7. The stock is strained of the bones and vegetables, then strained through cloth.

ROASTED **PEACHES** WITH CRÈME FRAÎCHE AND MINT

I'M MORE OF A SAVORY COOK AND LIKE TO KEEP MY DESSERTS simple. When peaches are in season—here in Ohio our stone fruit hits its peak in August—there's no need to cover them up in a pie or a cobbler. Simply quarter them, dust them with sugar, and roast them with some butter till they're lightly caramelized and hot all the way through. It's crucial to use high heat (and convection if you have it) to compensate for the high moisture content of the fruit. Serve with crème fraîche, a squeeze of lime to brighten it, and some aromatic mint for color and flavor. If it happens to be hot the day you serve roasted peaches, offer vanilla ice cream instead of the crème fraîche.

I usually plan on serving half a large peach or one small peach per person. I like to peel the peaches because they're more elegant that way, but this is an optional step. To peel them, bring a large pot of water to a boil and prepare an ice bath (half ice, half water). Cut a shallow X into the bottom of each peach, drop the peaches into the boiling water for 60 seconds, and then remove them to the ice bath. The skins will peel off easily if the fruit is fresh.

2 large peaches or 4 small peaches, peeled or unpeeled

(as you prefer), pitted, and quartered

Sugar for dusting

2 tablespoons/30 grams butter

½ cup/120 milliliters crème fraîche

1 fat lime wedge (you'll need about 2 teaspoons lime juice)

5 to 10 mint leaves, cut in a chiffonade

SERVES 4

- **PREHEAT** the oven to 425°F/220°C (or 400°F/200°C if you have convection).

- **SPRINKLE** the peaches all over with sugar as you would season meat with salt. In a heavy, ovenproof skillet, **MELT** the butter over medium-high heat. When the butter is melted, **PUT** the peaches in the pan with one of the cut sides down. **PUT** the pan in the oven and **ROAST** for 10 minutes. **TIP** the peaches onto the other cut side and continue to **COOK** until they're nicely browned, another 5 minutes or so (if you leave them in the oven too long they'll be too mushy).

- **DIVIDE** the peaches between four bowls. **PUT** a quenelle, or dollop, of crème fraîche on top of each, **SQUEEZE** a little lime juice over the bowls, and **GARNISH** with the mint chiffonade. **SERVE** immediately.

Step 1. After submerging the peaches in boiling water for 60 seconds, plunge them into an ice bath till they're totally chilled.

Step 2. Fresh ripe peaches peel easily, like this; under-ripe peaches don't peel easily.

Step 3. Making an X in the bottom before blanching makes the peeling easier.

Step 4. Peaches and mint, which grow at the same time of year, are a lovely pair.

Step 5. Start the peaches in a hot, heavy pan in a little butter, cut side down.

Step 6. Turn and finish roasting in a hot oven.

ROASTED PINEAPPLE
WITH VANILLA ICE CREAM AND CARAMEL SAUCE

WHEN I WORKED AT THE FRENCH LAUNDRY ON ITS NAMESAKE cookbook, the pastry chef, Stephen Durfee, served a pineapple "chop"—a hat tip to the endlessly inventive chef David Burke, who created the restaurant's salmon "chop." The salmon and the pineapple were cut into chop shapes, with the skin serving as the "bone" in both cases. The pineapple in particular made a lovely "rack," with the stiff green skin resembling an entire rack of lamb.

What stays with me, though, is how good cooked pineapple is. It roasts beautifully, doing what roasted things are meant to do—namely, develop rich complex flavors. The tart pineapple, rich ice cream, and sweet caramel sauce are a perfect combination, and I love the hot-cold nature of the dessert. Feel free to roast and slice the pineapple up to 3 hours in advance and keep it covered at room temperature; rewarm it in a hot oven just before serving.

Try finishing roasted fruits with a delicate amount of freshly ground black pepper; we think of spiciness mainly for savory dishes, but the same spiciness balances the sweetness of most fruit.

1 pineapple

2 tablespoons granulated sugar

¼ cup/60 grams butter

½ cup/100 grams brown sugar

¼ cup/60 milliliters cream

8 scoops vanilla ice cream

SERVES 8

- **PREHEAT** the oven to 425°F/220°C (or 400°F/200°C if you have convection).

- **REMOVE** the top and bottom of the pineapple, and **PEEL** it. **CUT** the pineapple into quarters lengthwise and **REMOVE** the core from each quarter. **CUT** each quarter in half widthwise so that you have 8 pieces. **SEASON** the pieces all over with the granulated sugar.

- In a heavy, ovenproof skillet, **MELT** the butter over medium-high heat. When the butter is melted, **PUT** the pineapple pieces into the pan with one of the cut sides down. **PUT** the pan in the oven and **ROAST** for 10 minutes. **TIP** the pineapples onto their other cut sides and continue to **COOK** until they're nicely browned, another 5 minutes or so.

- While the pineapple is roasting, **PUT** the brown sugar in a small, high-sided saucepan along with just enough water to make the sugar look like wet sand. **COOK** over high heat until the water cooks off and the sugar froths and bubbles, 2 to 3 minutes; then **REDUCE** the heat to medium-low and **COOK** for another minute or so. **ADD** the cream in a steady stream (be careful—it will boil violently on contact with the melted brown sugar) and **STIR** to incorporate.

- **SERVE** the roasted pineapple on the skin but sliced from it and cut into bite-size pieces, as in the photos, topped with the ice cream and drizzled with the warm caramel sauce.

EQUIPMENT &
TOOLS

THE OVEN

I am not *Consumer Reports,* and there are too many ovens with too many features to evaluate meaningfully in this book. I will say that many appliance makers make terrible decisions that confuse the consumer. I have a friend who has a stove allowing her to choose between "convection bake" or "convection roast," for instance. I saw another with a selection called "extended bake," and even the salesman had no idea what it meant. On the other hand, some ovens offer a "proof" setting that keeps the oven at 90°F/30°C to 125°F/52°C, which is a feature I would love for proofing bread and making yogurt.

One important consideration that Donna insisted I address when we bought our range is that it have a self-cleaning function. This is especially important if you're going to roast, since roasting requires high heat. Hot fat combined with juices from meat or moist fruits and vegetables will cause the fat to splatter, resulting in mists of grease spreading to all surfaces of your oven every time you roast. Furthermore, animal fat smokes at high temperatures, so in order to keep the smoke level low in your kitchen when roasting meat, you need a clean oven. A self-cleaning oven is a must in our house since cleaning by hand is something we don't want to do weekly. (This convenience does come with a caveat: some cooks have reported electrical issues due to the heavy electrical demands of the self-cleaning function, so the make of your oven and the configuration of your fuse box may be an issue.)

Gas versus electric is another question you need to answer. Some self-cleaning ovens require dual-fuel outputs—that is, gas burners on the stovetop (far, far superior to electric coils) and an electric oven. There's not a huge difference between gas and electric ovens in terms of roasting—they both get the cooking box hot. But it's generally acknowledged (usually by bakers) that a gas-fueled oven results in a more humid environment, while an electric oven has a drier but more uniform heat. Dryness has a bigger impact on baked goods, for which humidity is desirable, than on roasted foods, where the difference is not so noticeable. That said, uniformity of temperature is an advantage to the cook roasting the evening's dinner, so I would (and did) choose an electric oven with gas burners.

Other than those issues, the features of different ovens are a matter of preference and cost.

ROTISSERIE ROASTING

I'm a big fan of rotisserie roasting. It is the oldest form of roasting we know, probably dating to our earliest days as emergent *Homo sapiens* and lasting till the advent of ready coal and cast iron in the late eighteenth century—that is, until just moments ago in the grand scheme of things. When I cook meat over an open fire I feel in my heart a connection with all the roasters who came before me—I feel especially human. This may sound melodramatic, but there it is.

Granted, I have the luxury of a big fire pit; it's harder to feel connected with the cooks of the Middle Ages roasting meats (and themselves) before giant fires when you've got a gas Weber and a little battery-operated spit. But still: no matter how the heat is applied, turning meat on a spit is a superlative cooking method. The meat heats evenly and achieves good caramelization all over as fat rendering out of the skin bastes that skin and meat while it turns. I bought an electric rotisserie for fifty dollars because that's what worked for my situation. Evaluate your needs and search for what's available (usually the simpler, the better). If you want to use it when camping, for instance, get a battery-powered rotisserie; if you have a specific make of grill you want to use, stick with that company and use their attachments.

ROASTING VESSELS

The best roasting vessel by far is the cast-iron skillet. You can certainly buy them new, but you can also often find them at yard sales and antique stores. To clean an old cast-iron skillet, put it in the oven when you turn on the self-clean mode; this gets rid of decades of cooked-on fat. After that, just keep it well oiled, known as "seasoning." The low sides allow circulation around whatever you're roasting, and you can start or finish the dish on the stovetop. But any skillet will do, provided it doesn't have a nonstick coating or a plastic handle. If you have pans with handles that will melt in the oven, I recommend you throw them out or regift them to someone you'd prefer to see less of.

For larger items I roast on a baking sheet (put some parchment down first for easy cleanup). Again, the low sides allow for greater circulation. If the item is too large for a skillet and will release a lot of fat, you'd best use a roasting pan, but this is not a necessary vessel to have. Of course I use a roasting pan when forced to cook a humongous turkey; I also roast potatoes in a roasting pan when I'm cooking for a group. But that's about it. And I don't use a roasting rack, either. Yes, a rack will keep the meat from sticking to the bottom, but I usually like that (with a roasted chicken, for instance).

As most of the photos in this book show, I roast in circular vessels that I can also put over a flame on the stovetop.

ROASTING TOOLS

There are five tools that I consider mandatory for roasting.

1 SIDE TOWELS for taking hot pans out of the oven. Any heavy-duty towel will do, though I prefer sturdy, large (typically 1½ by 2 feet/45 by 60 centimeters) cloths that, when folded, give you good leverage on the handle of a hot pan—just make sure you keep them dry! A Google search will give you options; I'm partial to the ones I began using at the CIA, which offers them for sale online. I find potholders hopelessly clunky and inefficient, but if that's what you're used to, OK. (It's an uphill battle of mine, to rid the world of potholders, but I try. Same with oven mitts; I won't comment further in the spirit of if-you-can't-say-something-nice, but they're even worse than potholders for hindering your movement and control.)

2 A THERMOMETER to monitor the internal temperature of the meat. An inexpensive instant-read digital thermometer from the hardware store will work and is great for smaller cuts. Be sure to warm the probe before putting it into the meat; if it's cold you might not get an accurate reading. Better still, I favor a cable thermometer, which allows you to monitor the internal temperature of a roast without opening the oven. I cherish my iGrill thermometer, which sends the temperature reading to my iPhone via Bluetooth. I do not recommend those old analog meat thermometers, though I grew up with one. Their readings are not exact, and they often come printed with outdated temperature recommendations.

3 A LARGE, FLAT-EDGED, WOODEN SPOON. This serves two purposes when I'm roasting (in addition to its myriad purposes on the stovetop). I use it to lift heavy roasted items—whether by sticking it into the cavity of a bird or using two to lift from below. And I use it to deglaze pans, scraping up skin and other delicious browned stuff that has stuck to the bottom. Whenever I travel to cook, these are among the first items I pack in my kit.

4 **A SHARP KNIFE.** I repeat: a *sharp* knife. I maintain that the number one problem in American home kitchens is dull knives. A dull knife makes your work harder and mutilates your beautifully roasted food. I urge you to purchase two good knives (a chef's knife and a paring knife) and then find a good wet-grind knife-sharpening service near you. My favorite knife-sharpening device for the home is the DMT sharpening "stone," which is actually a perforated, diamond-coated metal sheet that works wonders in between professional sharpenings. A gift certificate for professional knife sharpening is also a great gift to give the cook in your family. I've noted it before, but it bears repeating: nothing says "I love you" like a really sharp knife.

5 **A BIG, HEAVY CUTTING BOARD** for carving roasted meats (using your lightning-sharp knife) after they've rested. I couldn't get by without a big board for everyday cooking and a second big board with a moat around it to catch the inevitable juices.

BEYOND THESE FIVE, I wouldn't want to be without butcher's string, but it's certainly possible to roast without it. An oven thermometer to gauge the temperature of your oven can be useful if your oven seems to be misbehaving. Vessels of various shapes and sizes, basting spoons (I especially love my offset spoons), and of course any of the silly and/or useful doodads and gizmos found at cookware stores worldwide—I leave their relative "necessity" to be determined by the preferences and budget of the one doing the roasting.

THE ROASTING
LARDER

• **KOSHER SALT** is the salt I reach for most in my kitchen. I buy Morton's because it's what's available at my grocery store, but Diamond Crystal is more popular among chefs. As far as I'm concerned, the most important issue with salt choice is that you consistently use the same kind. All salts have different weights by volume and crystal size; because we salt by sight and feel, the amount you can hold between all your fingers and thumb differs between brands. So use whatever you like best—kosher salt or sea salt, coarse or fine, any brand—just be sure you always use the same kind.

• **FAT** is usually generated by the process of roasting, but often I put down a film of oil in the pan to minimize sticking. When I do, it's always vegetable oil, which is economical and has a high smoke point. I don't use olive oil in roasting at very high heat because it can take on bitter flavors (and is more expensive anyway), but you can if you wish. Butter will burn if the temperature is too hot, but it's a great finishing fat thanks to the added flavor of the butter solids. I use salted butter because that's what I'm used to; you can use either salted or unsalted as long as you use them consistently.

• BLACK PEPPER is a good seasoning for almost anything roasted. Buy whole peppercorns and keep them in a decent pepper mill so you can grind it fresh as you need it. You can enhance the flavor of black peppercorns by a factor of ten by toasting them before grinding them. It may not be practical all the time, but it offers a great demonstration of the impact of heating whole dried spices.

• CORIANDER is by far my favorite spice. I use it all the time, often combined with black pepper, which is great on most roasted meats (indeed, the black crust you see on pastrami is usually a straight mix of crushed black pepper and crushed coriander). I don't know when coriander has ever harmed a dish. As with most spices, coriander is best bought whole and then crushed in a mortar or beneath a sauté pan as needed. (I use it so often that I really should invest in another grinder just for this.) Again, the A-student in the kitchen always toasts a spice before grinding it.

• FRESH HERBS grow in my backyard all spring, summer, and fall. I love being able to walk out the back door, knife in hand, and return with a bunch of chives or parsley or sage or rosemary. And especially thyme. I love thyme and find that it's especially suited to roasting. Toss a bunch into the cooking fat for added flavor as you baste the meat. (It's also lovely to look at.)

It should be noted here that herbs are divided into two categories, soft and hard. A soft herb is a leaf or shoot, such as parsley, chives,

Roast with hard herbs,
finish with soft.

tarragon, cilantro, or any herb that does not grow from a thick or woody stem. Hard herbs include oregano, rosemary, and even thyme, though some varieties have delicate stems. Soft herbs should always be used at the end of the cooking or to finish something that has been cooked, since their flavor is too volatile to withstand long periods in high heat. Hard herbs, on the other hand, work well in high heat, which is why adding chopped oregano early in the cooking of a tomato sauce has great impact, whereas adding basil early on has virtually none.

• **DRIED HERBS** are valuable, but time is required to release their flavor. If I have been a diligent gardener and cook, I've harvested my herbs in the fall, allowed them to dry on the counter, and then stored them in plastic containers or zipper-top plastic bags in the freezer for use throughout the winter. Herbs you grow and dry yourself are superior to store-bought dried herbs in terms of flavor and strength—and they're much less expensive, too.

• **GARLIC** is not well understood in the kitchen, I've found. Super strong when raw, its power is quickly dispelled in heat. So use plenty and use it with abandon. Crush it lightly so that its interior is exposed but it remains in one piece, and add it to the cooking fat you're basting your meat with as it roasts. It's a fabulous flavoring device.

• **ONION** is such a powerful force in the kitchen that I think of it more as a tool than an ingredient. Depending on how you cook it, it adds sweetness and depth to any savory dish. Sweat the onion lightly and it adds one flavor; cook it till it's brown and it adds a different flavor—or, more precisely, *flavors,* plural, as the cooked sugars become more complex and varied. Add it raw to a stock and it adds still another. Macerate it in vinegar and it's a different ingredient altogether. Learn how to manipulate the onion and you become a better cook. Roasted onions make a great side dish, too, come to think of it.

ACKNOWLEDGMENTS

FIRST, THANKS GO TO MY WIFE AND PARTNER, DONNA.
Without her images, my books would be lesser by more than half, as we both work hard to convey information through the images rather than create highly stylized food photography. I like pretty food, and food should look enticing, but my first impulse is to show you what food can and should look like in your kitchen, and Donna conveys exactly this. I've cooked all the dishes in this book at home and Donna has photographed them here as well.

My chief recipe tester, over the course of many years and many books, is Marlene Newell, who runs the site cookskorner.com. Sticklers for detail and precision, she and her team of cooks ensure that all the recipes make sense and work. I can't imagine doing a book without her.

Karen Wise is the copy editor of this book; she is true to her name and copyedits most everything I write.

Michael Sand, an executive editor at Little, Brown, is responsible for bringing this series into being, and for this and his sage counsel, I am grateful. As I am for the whole Little, Brown team that labors on my behalf: Deborah Jacobs, Cathy Gruhn, Meghan Deans, and their staffs as well.

I'm thrilled to be working with David and Joleen Hughes, of Level, who have determined the entire look and feel of this book, from colors to fonts to graphics to the way all these elements, including the photography, come together.

Emilia Juocys is my assistant, but I'm never comfortable with that term as it doesn't encompass the extent of Emilia's work or describe our relationship. She helps test and develop recipes, keeps me organized, serves as a kind of personal trainer in generating my work, and generally saves my ass on pretty much a weekly basis.

This book is dedicated to Peter Stevenson, a fellow writer and one of my oldest and dearest friends. Peter gave me a place to stay when my work required me to be in Manhattan, as it did frequently over the years, and I'd have been unable to afford to take on that work without his ongoing generosity. Long overdue thanks to you, Peter.

INDEX

Page numbers in *italics* refer to photographs.

ABOUT THE AUTHOR

Michael Ruhlman's innovative and successful food reference books include *Egg: A Culinary Exploration of the World's Most Versatile Ingredient*, *Ratio*, *The Elements of Cooking, Ruhlman's Twenty*, and *Charcuterie*. He has appeared as a judge on *Iron Chef America* and as a featured guest on Anthony Bourdain's *No Reservations*. He has also coauthored books with Thomas Keller, Eric Ripert, and Michael Symon. He lives in Cleveland with his wife, photographer Donna Turner Ruhlman, and their two children.